RESPECTING
Residential
Work *with*
Children

By James R. Harris Jr., M.A.

Respecting Residential Work With Children

Copyright©2003
James R. Harris, Jr.

All rights are reserved under international and Pan-American copyright conventions. No part of this publication may be reproduced, stored in a retrieval system, or transmitted in any form or by any means, electronic, mechanical, photocopying, recording, scanning, or otherwise, except as permitted under Section 107 or 108 of the 1976 United States Copyright Act, without either the prior express written permission of the author or publisher or authorization through payment of the appropriate per-copy fee, except for brief quotations in critical reviews.

Limit of liability/Disclaimer of Warranty: While the publisher and author have used their best efforts in preparing this book, they make no representations or warranties with respect to the accuracy or completeness of the contents of this book and specifically disclaim any implied warranties of merchantability or fitness for a particular purpose. No warranty may be created or extended by sales representative or written sales materials. The advice and strategies contained herein may not be suitable for your situation. You should consult with a professional where appropriate. Neither the publisher nor author shall be liable for any loss or profit a or any other commercial damages, including but not limited to special, incidental, consequential, or other damages.

Published by
NEARI Press
70 North Summer Street
Holyoke, MA 01040
413.540.0712

Distributed by
Whitman Distribution
10 Water Street
PO Box 1220
Lebanon, New Hampshire 03766
603.448.0037
800.353.3730

ISBN# 1-929657- 21 - 8

Price US $ 35.00

ENDORSEMENTS FOR RESPECTING RESIDENTIAL WORK WITH CHILDREN

Jim Harris is an important new contributor to child welfare literature. He understands how to work with children in residential care. He also knows how to work within the complex, sometimes troubled system that protects these kids. This expansion into the broader systems view of care makes *Respecting Residential Work With Children* one of the most insightful observations of children's treatment systems. We all should be reading Jim Harris.

Jerry Hatfield, LCDP, Associate Professor of Human Services, Community College of Rhode Island. and author of *Preparing for Human Services Work* and *Basic Field Skills for Human Service Workers*.

This book is easy to read and very informative regarding the expectations of residential staffing. It was nice to see points that we at New Hope for Children make to our staff on a daily basis be confirmed by others in the field.

Robert Nix, Executive Director
New Hope For Children

Having personally worked with (and advocated for) troubled children for nearly four decades, I appreciate Jim Harris' commitment to youth in care as evidenced in *Respecting Residential Work With Children*. Being a state legislator, I have known Jim for five years and attest that he truly cares about children in care, and the staff who work them. This book demonstrates this commitment. It is a sound reference for all who choose to work with youth in residential placement.

Representative Maxine Shavers, Deputy Majority Leader, Rhode Island House of Representatives.

Respecting Residential Work With Children is a window into Jim Harris' expertise regarding the needs of children in residential placement. The author's dedication to improve the quality of care and quality of life for these youth is evident throughout this book. Jim provides outstanding insight, ideas for sound practice, and his work is an excellent resource for residential staff members!

Cindy Bacon, R.I. Department of Children, Youth and Families: Licensing Division

For Laurie,
for all the love, encouragement and support
you have given in all things I have ever done.

ACKNOWLEDGEMENTS

There are many people I need to thank for helping make this publication a reality.

Jerry Hatfield of the *Community College of Rhode Island* was the first person to review this work. He felt the manuscript had potential and encouraged me to go forward. I am deeply appreciative of Jerry for his support of this book, and for his commitment to the human services field – including those who work in children's residential programs.

Rob Longo of *New Hope Treatment Centers* in South Carolina was the first person outside of Rhode Island to read the text. Being such an important contributor to the field, it was gratifying to learn of his interest in my manuscript. Rob gave excellent feedback and brought the book to the point of publication. I am truly honored to have the support of Rob Longo. His belief in my work means a lot.

There are two other professionals I want thank for their help with final adjustments to the text. Floyd Alwon of the *Child Welfare League of America* provided valuable criticism and ways to make the book better. I have always admired Floyd and am appreciative that someone of his stature took the time to become involved with this book. Charlie Appelstein who gave us the fictional character Gus E. Studelmeyer, striking a chord in our field with the *Gus Chronicles,* also gave me important suggestions. He encouraged me not to shy away from some of the tougher issues stating, "You are writing what many people think." I appreciate Charlie's insight and support.

I am appreciative of Ernest Campagnone, a professional who has devoted his career to making children's residential programs better. When we tried to establish a training curriculum for direct care workers in Rhode Island, Ernie was the first to offer his assistance. He taught me so much about milieu therapy and systemic issues. People like Ernie inspire us to be the best that we can be (for the kids).

Deb Lilli, an English professor at the *Community College of Rhode Island,* spent a good deal of time editing this text and I am thankful for her guidance.

Steve Bengis is the CEO of the *New England Adolescent Research Institute* (NEARI) who published this book. I am indebted to Steve for providing me with this opportunity.

Of course I would be remiss if I did not thank my wife. Laurie is one of the best childcare workers I have ever known. She was instrumental in my finishing this book, sacrificing many evenings in 2002 while I worked away in the den (many times late into the night). Her understanding of my work was paramount to its completion.

Lastly, I want to thank all the children I have ever worked with in residential placement. Their resiliency has always been a source of inspiration to me.

TABLE OF CONTENTS

FOREWORD XII
INTRODUCTION XIII

CHAPTER ONE

Milieu Therapy 1

Residential milieus and therapeutic communities: brief histories 2
Some working definitions..5
Basic milieu musts..8
Establishing safety in the milieu 9
The impact of the physical environment 13
The unconditional belief of one adult 15
The chance to promote change 17

CHAPTER TWO

Roles 19

Lack of internal communication 19
Roles within an agency..21
Direct care staff...22
Residential supervisors/program managers.....................24
Clinicians..26
Residential program types 28
Keeping expectations about our work in check 30

CHAPTER THREE

Behavior Management 32

Biological bases of behavior 32
The impact of abuse and neglect on the brain................35

Meeting needs 36
Verbal interventions utilized in behavior management 39
Logical consequences...41
Physical interventions..45
Questioning your behavior management program.....................46

CHAPTER FOUR

Human Stage Development 48

Three textbook views bring us to the present day.....................48
Erikson still makes sense..49
The new American culture 51
Erikson's eight stages 52
Cognitive theory – Piaget...54
Piaget's stages of cognitive development 55
Kohlberg and moral development 57
Applying moral development to children in residential placement 58
Different learning styles in youth 59
Wrapping it all up 60

CHAPTER FIVE

Issues of Grief, Loss and Trauma 62

Grief and loss for children in care..62
Ways to help children cope 63
Being a good listener 65
Creativity can be used to express feelings...................................66
Symptoms of trauma..68
Post traumatic stress disorder...70
Symptoms of PTSD 71
Managing PTSD symptoms within the milieu 74
Secondary trauma – compassion fatigue....................................75
Tips for (staff) stress reduction..76
Next steps...77

CHAPTER SIX

Working With The Families of Children in Care 78

Don't condemn a child's parents..78
Adoption and Safe Families Act of 1997 81
Family preservation 84
Reunification and permanence is not ideal in all families 87
Paternal deprivation 89
Advocating for children and families: new thinking 90

CHAPTER SEVEN

Establishing Diversity in the Milieu..91

Cultural competence in our work...91
Cultural competence thwarted 94
Assessing an agency's practice of cultural competence....................95
Changing with the times..96
The changing face of American ethnicity 97
What do the numbers tell us about children in care?.....................98
Making the milieu reflective of the ethnic diversity of all children.....100
Culture as it defines children in residential placement..................102
Jeffrey the little African American boy who thought he was Italian.......104
All of us are just people helping people 106

CHAPTER EIGHT

Ethics In Our Field: Do We Walk The Walk? 107

The walls of silence 107
Our walls of silence 108
One true story..110
Fear + confusion = cover ups?...112
Ethical codes in the child care profession 113
Ethics in the agency and children's rights 118
Accepting that children have the right to be loved 122
Final thoughts on ethics in our field..123

CHAPTER NINE

The Workforce Crisis 124

Don't fear the future..125
RI initiatives to raise program budgets and professionalize our field 127
Staff development, certification, and conferences 128
How do we bring a team approach to residential placement? 131
Where do we go from here?..132

CHAPTER TEN

Educational Needs for Children in Care 134

Current Trends in the Education of Children and Youth in Care........134
Looking Past a Child's Behavior to Ensure Their Education 136
Schools and Residential Treatment Agencies 138
Promising Practices to Address Deficient Areas 142
The Future Can Be As Bright As We Want It To Be For Youth in Care ...143

FINAL THOUGHTS 144

APPENDIX

Additional Resources 147

BIBLIOGRAPHY 153

ABOUT THE AUTHOR 163

FOREWORD

I am quite fortunate to have worked closely with Jim Harris on a number of interesting projects over the years. Jim's heartfelt desire to improve the quality of life for children in out-of-home care is recognized and admired by all who know him. Readers will feel this concern throughout this book.

Jim wrote this book to provide a useful tool for front-line direct care workers, a tool that was not available to him or his peers when they began working with troubled children. In this book, Jim sets forth an easy-to-understand overview of the major theories and treatment philosophies that underlie the "therapeutic milieu." Here the new worker will find a good orientation to the best writers and thinkers. References to the original works are provided for those wishing to pursue the subject matter in greater depth.

Supervisors and others responsible for the orientation and training of new workers will find much helpful information throughout this book. Many of the chapters could serve as the basis for thought provoking, in-service staff development sessions.

Like many leaders in the field, Jim realized quite some time ago that we needed to improve the competence and professional status of the child and youth care worker. He understands that a trained and competent workforce is the single most important cornerstone in the development of a healthy service delivery system. Unlike many other leaders however, Jim has held true to his beliefs. He continues to promote this vision of the professional direct care worker with a missionary zeal. Through this book, Jim provides a practical contribution that supports this vision.

Floyd Alwon, Ed.D.
Director
Walker Trieschman National Center for Professional Development
Child Welfare League of America

November 25, 2002

INTRODUCTION

The greatest challenge in writing this manuscript was to find another way to relate to residential programming staff, particularly the direct care worker. Some books are so technical that they just cannot be used as an everyday resource. Others are too simplistic. My attempt with this book was to weave experiential insight, theory, and current initiatives into a text that respects the intelligence of children's residential programming staff. The intent of this work is to not only help the reader understand the basics in residential programming, but also to stimulate critical thinking amongst those in our field.

As you read this book you will notice it is complete with concepts, theory, personal experiences, and historical insight. This may not be your standard text. The chapters are segmented so the reader can identify those topics most important to them. The book is also full of vignettes, citations and codes. In fact, the ethical code I included in chapter eight serves as a model for our work with children. Psychologists and social workers have their own codes. Why shouldn't our field have its own code? Chapter five incorporates attributes for "good listening skills." These inclusions (amongst many) were written to make this book a practical resource, one that can be referenced time and time again.

There are some important points I would like to make regarding this text:

1. When I set out to write this book it was intended to be for the direct care worker. While the final product is suited for these workers, especially those new to children's residential programming, I also think that line supervisors can take something from this text.

2. Some of the examples utilized in this book actually occurred. Others are a combination of incidents I've learned of. They may, or may not be, case studies from my personal experiences. These examples serve to reiterate points. They can also be utilized for discussion purposes during agency staff meetings or trainings.

3. I tried to be as honest as I could in this text. At times, this resulted in my preaching to the choir. On other occasions I am strongly challenging that choir. It is my belief that our field doesn't do enough in terms of internal exploration of the system (good or bad). Only by admitting what we do well – and what we do not do well enough - can we adjust our services and move forward in this rapidly changing world.

I am a former direct care worker who has not forgotten his roots. I am also an administrator, advocate, lobbyist, workshop facilitator, historian, sports enthusiast, and researcher. All of these voices come out in the book. Instead of trying to stop some or curtail others, I tried to find a way to use all of them. This is because our jobs in the residential setting require us to wear many hats. We are role models, mechanics, teachers, carpenters, parents, transporters, administrative assistants (completing paperwork is part of the job), and the list goes on and on.

One thing that I am passionate about is that those who work with children in residential programs hold one of the more important jobs in our society. Residential staff members have the chance to help wounded children and fractured families. Sure, the pay might not be great, and the community may not give us enough credit. But we have to look at what we do receive: the chance to work with some really special kids. We can go to bed at night knowing that we have made the most of our day. And while we acknowledge that gratification within our jobs comes in small increments, we are making a difference in the world – one day, and one child at a time.

All of us who devote our professional lives to helping youth in residential placement have essential jobs. I only hope that this text helps in some small way, both as a resource and to stimulate critical thinking within our profession.

James R. Harris, Jr., M.A.
November 26, 2002

CHAPTER ONE
Milieu Therapy

"The best prize that life offers is the chance to work hard at something worth doing."

Theodore Roosevelt

The field of children's residential work is not one that receives its fair share of attention in our society. Those of us who work in the profession accept the fact that the intrinsic rewards we receive will far outweigh the low pay and lack of public recognition. I once heard it said that, "the greatest thing a person can give aside from their love, is their labor." Those who work in our field give both. That is why working with children in residential placement is one of the most underrated professions in all of America.

Residential facilities have helped thousands of children transcend horrific pasts to realize brighter futures. Our work is tiring, demanding, but it is still a job worth doing. These children's future and our future are at stake with each youngster that walks through the front door of a residential facility. In helping these children, we are, in turn, helping society. We are making an investment in our own future and the future of America.

Throughout history there have always been children who have lived apart from their families. These youth were provided places to eat and sleep, but they were never treated in the "clinical" sense until the middle of the 20th century. Today, there are more children than ever living in residential facilities. One influence that makes our jobs more complex is the need to now balance politics, psychology, financial resources, and mandated state policies within these programs. Additionally, the children's clinical issues are multifaceted. This makes our jobs more difficult than they have ever been in the past.

There are growing volumes of literature available on the subject of residential work with children. However, the earliest years of this profession were not well documented. This somewhat *foggy* (literary) history paints the landscape of a profession that simply sprouted up to meet a need. It all began when individuals began to feel that children in care should not just be provided the basic necessities. They should also have the chance to heal their wounds.

RESIDENTIAL MILIEUS AND THERAPEUTIC COMMUNITIES: BRIEF HISTORIES

During World War II a concept previously utilized in Europe for over a century in the treatment of emotionally wounded soldiers surfaced in America. The concept of care was labeled as "therapeutic community." It was based on the premise of "moral treatment" of the emotionally disturbed. Benjamin Rush had written extensively on the subject as far back as the 1860's. Simply stated, the moral therapist believed environmental factors played a significant role in the treatment process of the disturbed individual (Campagnone, In Press, 2002). Therefore, institutions were established in quiet community settings and well staffed, thereby satisfying many of the physical needs of the clients.

The therapeutic community design re-established many of the concepts of moral therapy. It was surmised that progress and rehabilitation were more effective when attention was paid to the milieu (therapeutic environment). To further advance the practice of moral therapy, a shift occurred. This new design incorporated the use of social systems and interpersonal relationships to provide emotional support during the primary period of stress (Campagnone, In Press, 2002). The therapeutic community demanded an open environment for communication and trust, contact with outside communities, and strong relationships with staff (Campagnone, In Press, 2002). Thus the establishment of "community" in the treatment setting became the goal for all programming.

Whenever discussions of our history occurs the therapeutic community design is a good place to start. Today, many programs incorporate numerous aspects of this programming philosophy. While the types of clients that we assist may have changed, this modality still seems to work. We do not always have to reinvent the wheel.

In the late 1960's Albert Trieschman, James Whittaker, and Larry Brendtro wrote the landmark text *The Other Twenty-Three Hours*. This publication is still "on the mark" and helpful to staff. It has been many people's introduction to residential work. The text offers the insight needed to begin working with minimal training. Trieschman, Whittaker and Brendtro (1969) affirm that a major goal of the milieu should be helping children change their negative behaviors to more acceptable ones. They assert:

> *We would like to help a child stop or diminish deviant, dangerous, age-inappropriate behavior. We would like to help him start or develop adaptive, productive, age-appropriate behavior. In short, we need to help the child to alter his behavior* (p.4).

To fully understand the role of the milieu in treatment a definition is needed. When referring to "milieu" in this text, it is intended to describe the residential environment in which children are placed. This can be the group home, residential treatment center, shelter, independent living program, or any other facility that provides services to children in out-of-home care. The next chapter of the text will discuss residential facility types.

Milieu therapy refers to any program that utilizes certain prescribed ways to achieve therapeutic ends (Campagnone, In Press, 2002). This is done through several areas of programming, structure, and communication, for example. It is not a specific modality in that different program designs emphasize various areas of the environment. The therapeutic community is a very special kind of milieu therapy. It operates on the principle that all social and interpersonal processes in the facility are relevant to therapy and that each and every person that works there is integral to the clients' treatment (Campagnone, In Press, 2002). The facility is, first and foremost, a social system in and of itself. It is influenced by people who are its members and by the surroundings.

A major component of this social system is a basic change in how providers deliver services to the client. In the traditional concept of care, the emotionally needy were often left sitting in day rooms or bedrooms waiting for someone to treat them (Campagnone, In Press, 2002). Most, if not all of these large institutions had an abundance of clients who had been there for years without improvement. This newer therapeutic community model is very exact in one concept - in some capacity, the clients themselves provide and receive "treatment" from other clients (Campag-none, In Press, 2002). It requires residents to act and evaluate each other. Thus, the provider of service becomes the community at large. This principle exists in varying degrees in all therapeutic communities.

Because members of the therapeutic community are assessing and evaluating each other's actions, they should also be discussing them at community meetings. With proper guidance and dialogue, the end product results in the clients' involvement in their treatment, planning, and daily functioning. It also provides the basis for the social system the group will live under. This will hopefully provide the clients with opportunities to experiment newly learned social behaviors and thoughts in a safe and trusted environment (Campagnone, In Press, 2002).

The premise of the facility, being a small community in its own right, is important. It gives the clients a chance to practice strategies and behaviors. It also allows them to make mistakes that will be addressed by this smaller community (Campagnone, In Press, 2002). That is why this area of treatment is so vital. It allows the clients an opportunity in a "win-win" situation. It is a safe place to experiment with real life situations.

This notion of the milieu being its own "small community" is summed up nicely in the University of Oklahoma's *Training Course for Residential Workers* (1986):

> *The residential setting is an ecological (natural/environmental) setting composed of developing human beings – staff, co-workers and the children. All are interacting with each other and with the daily changes in the setting of the residence. By being totally aware of the setting, we can plan a system that will benefit the children* (Volume 3, p. 11).

In children's residential treatment, the need for community must include the involvement of the clients' parent(s) whenever possible. Regardless of what we may think of a child's parents, they are still important in that youngster's life. We do not have the right to take that away. (This is covered in greater detail in chapter six.) In *Parents of Children in Placement: Perspective and Programs* (1988), Paula Sinanoglu and Anthony Maluccio contend that programs must incorporate working with a child's parents into the client's treatment plan. This text, a decade and a half old, was chosen to show that we are still laboring in attempts to include family work in our service delivery. Sinanoglu and Maluccio (1988), proclaim that:

> *Residential placement centers should be a resource for parents, along with the active participation of parents in the program of*

the center. Staff should recognize the importance of parents to the child as well as the parents' own needs and mobilize the agency and community resources on behalf of the parents and the family as a whole (p.7).

The other issue of great importance in residential placement is recognizing the role that the outside community plays and the importance in utilizing these environments in our treatment of youth. These settings include school, campus activities (in the larger programs), little league, girl scouts, church, and so on. Children in care need to experience these environments to understand that they are not simply closed in a world that provides them treatment and keeps them from the outside community. This is extremely important because one day these youth will be returning home, become adopted, etc., and will be immersed in the outside community. Agencies, and staff members, must make sure that such community involvement is a major part of the milieu therapy. This will be discussed in various chapters throughout the text.

Some Working Definitions Applicable to Children's Residential Work

Milieu Therapy refers to any program that utilizes aspects of the environment in specified or prescribed ways to achieve therapeutics ends (Campagnone, 2002). This means that the residential facility takes advantage of all aspects of the setting in its treatment of children.

Therapeutic Community is a form of milieu therapy that operates on the principle that all of the social and interpersonal processes in the unit are relevant to therapy and should be used therapeutically. Therapeutic community is based on the premise that the unit it encompasses is a social system. (Campagnone, 2002).

Integration of Services means that all services are incorporated within the structure. This includes residential and clinical treatment. It is also extended to include educational services in some programs. In addition, the integration encompasses a team approach to treatment. All staff work as one.

Therapy is a process of change. The definition also includes activities that are therapeutic in nature – in that the activity can aid in generating change.

In milieu therapy, it is important to realize this more encompassing definition of therapy. It is not to the child's advantage to receive only the standard one-hour of therapy per week in a clinician's office. We must utilize every opportunity available to help youth in residential treatment. Consider the youth's time spent with staff in a single year (8,760 hours):

TRADITIONALCLINICAL TIME..78 hours
(assumes 1.5 hours each week: does not deduct for clinician vacation/missed sessions)
SCHOOL TIME...1,680 hours
(assumes 7 hours a day, 35 hours a week, 48 weeks a year)
MILIEU TIME (Awake)...3,130 hours
(assumes 6.5 hours weekdays and 12 hours each week-end day x 48 weeks. Assumes
12 hours x four vacation weeks (weekdays only as week-ends already accounted for)
MILIEU TIME (Asleep)...3,872 hours
(assumes that the child is asleep at all times minus the three aforementioned times)

In reviewing this chart, it can be discerned that children spend less than 1% of their year in the traditional clinical setting. They spend just under 20% in a school setting. This means that 80% of the remaining time is spent in the milieu! And, at least half of that time is spent awake. Why wouldn't we want to make the most out of the "therapy time" that is available in the child's milieu? Agencies that recognize the role that direct care staff members play in a child's life develop truly integrative treatment plans for the youth in their charge. All agencies should make sure that at any time in a child's day (or night) there is an opportunity for treatment.

The notion of the direct care role being of primary importance should also translate into attendance at staff meetings. These workers should be invited, and expected, to be in attendance. It makes no sense for these folks to be absent from any meeting in which the *team* is discussing a child's treatment. This would be equivalent to a football team huddling up to call a play, without involving the offensive line. How would the linemen know what play was called and when the ball was being snapped? Obviously, the team would not be putting itself in position to do well. Likewise, the practice of not involving direct care staff in meetings is totally illogical. Those who spend the most time with youth in the milieu need to be at these meetings. (The role of staff members is discussed in greater detail in chapter two.)

The Milieu Environment
(Adapted from the work of Ernest Campagnone, In Press, 2002)

Each program/house is a special system and unique in its own right. It has its own characteristics, its own goals, its own values, and its own standards. By combining policy and procedures that address these issues a milieu program is developed. Each milieu program should attend to:
- *Open Communication*
- *Active Participation* of the members in treatment for each other. All must participate in making and monitoring *community* rules and guidelines.
- *Operation* of the community does not mean authority.

<u>The following are guidelines for any milieu program</u>:
- All therapy is rehabilitative – social expectations are maintained throughout.
- Everyone receives the same environment: the expectations are that of the community.
- Community is communal, no secrets. Honesty is critical.
- The central decision making forum is the community.
- Two-way communication – shared decision-making by those affected by decisions.
- Leadership is based on natural abilities rather than (simply) by titles.
- Significant roles within the community for everyone.

(continued next page)

> What milieu environments are supposed to do:
> 1. Provide safety, security and structure.
> 2. Provide emotional support.
> 3. Reeducate/train.
> 4. Provide and maintain a healthy reference group.
> 5. Encourage and support healthy behavior.
> 6. Most Important: develop a set of expectations for daily living/social functioning.

Basic Milieu Musts

The aforementioned examines the goals we should strive towards when working with youth in the milieu. In order to actualize these goals there are some basic principles that should be applied by all staff to all residential placement settings:

- *Put yourself in the child's shoes:* Would you make your six-year-old child do his/her own laundry, vacuum the rugs, and/or endlessly sit in a time-out?

- *A clean tidy house says a lot:* Often, children in residential placement come from disheveled settings. A messy and dirty environment could replicate the home that the state said was unfit for the child to live in. There is no excuse for a dirty milieu environment – and it's not the children's (sole) responsibility to clean the residence. (This is covered in greater detail later in this chapter.)

- *It's the child's needs, not staffs':* On February 3, 2002 the New England Patriots played in the Super Bowl. I heard the story of a group home that wouldn't let two of their residents (big Patriots fans) go to a program-wide Super Bowl party because they (the staff) didn't like football. They didn't want to get stuck watching a game all night long. Things like this should never be allowed to happen.

- *Children's residential work isn't for everyone:* This is a tough job for little pay. If workers are not thrilled at the thought of patiently and compassionately caring for troubled kids, this job isn't for them. And, there is no shame in this because there are plenty of other places to work that pay a better wage.

> *Children in care can experience "normal" childhoods:* They can go on vacations, celebrate holidays, participate in sporting leagues, join the cub scouts or girl scouts, go fishing, attend sporting events, and so forth. If we experienced these things in our childhood, and we let our biological children experience them, so should kids in care!

ESTABLISHING SAFETY IN THE MILIEU

One of the first things (in fact it is at the top of the list) that must be done in helping children in care is to assure their safety. Beliefs, values, program components, and milieu design should all encompass the safety of the clients. Children feel safe when they know that there is no present danger that will violate their physical or emotional integrity (Brohl, 1996). It is hard for children to work on their issues if they fear for their personal safety; if they feel they need eyes in the back of their heads (Seita, et al. 1996).

When working with children who have been abused or neglected, the task of assuring them that they are safe can be monumental. Staff members must be up to this challenge via sound training, agency support, and leaving all their misconceptions at the front door. This is because the children that we serve have their own special needs; they have their own beliefs about how and when safety is attained. Direct care staff must be willing to help the children meet safety needs (from the youths' perspective) and not the staff members' viewpoint. The following safety guide helps explain how this process can be established:

Guide To Establishing Safety For Residents In The Milieu

Many of the children served in residential programs have suffered abuse and/or neglect in one form or another. When staff is hired, especially those new to the field, the agency should provide an all-encompassing training program. Such training topics would include milieu therapy, child and adolescent stage development, behavior management, cultural diversity, the use of psychotropic medications, and other content areas reflective of an agency's programmatic structure. A new worker who is placed in the milieu without receiving any formalized training should be concerned. They should question the agency's values, beliefs, and commitment to quality care. (Even when programs are short staffed, it is still no excuse to send an untrained employee into the residential setting.)

Direct care workers should also expect support from its agency's executive and (especially) clinical teams. It is not unrealistic for upper level administrators and clinicians to visit the residence on occasion, interact with the youth, and participate in special events. If an agency's administrative and clinical teams never visit the milieu, this is not helpful. The same is true regarding weekend and school vacation weeks. If direct care staff are left on their own and expected to hold down the fort during these times, they are doing so without necessary supports, potentially reducing the quality of care.

New staff members should also be warned against bringing untested values and beliefs into the milieu. Some of these would include "we should shower these children with kindness" or "all the kids need is love." While staff members do connect with youth, these themes, especially if they are used to ignore destructive behavior, do not help children in care. In the eyes of many youngsters that we serve, *love* and *stability* mean that staff members must keep them safe. In many cases safety equates to structure and firm boundaries.

Role of Testing

Many youngsters in care have only experienced adult care as abusive and a danger to their well-being. Until staff members demonstrate that they are not like the adults in the child's past, children will be apprehensive around them. Through role modeling and showing that they care about how a child is feeling, staff members can help children feel a sense of safety. This process may take a long time.

Even when staff members set out to help define a child's needs, they may be unconsciously attempting to satisfy their own. When I first entered the field and heard stories about the horrific pasts of the children I was working with, I was stunned. My first thought was that I'd save these kids from the adults that hurt them. Fortunately, I listened to my peers, read as much material as I could get my hands on, and I learned that these youngsters did not want me to keep them from their family. They wanted me to keep them safe in the milieu.

The "testing phase" that every child goes through when first admitted to the program is of great importance. When a new child comes into the residence it is normal to experience a brief honeymoon period. While he or she becomes acquainted with the rules and routine of the house and gets to know other children and staff, they can be most compliant. Then their behavior can change. This is when staff must remember that *when children act out there is a reason behind it*. This is especially true in the case of children new to the milieu. They may be testing to see how staff responds to their behavior. It can easily be called the safety test.

If a staff member becomes angered, reacting in a loud threatening tone when a child breaks a rule, it might enable the youngster to hold onto the belief that *all* adults are abusive. On the other hand, the staff member who smiles and ignores the child's behavior (or nervously looks the other way) can convey a message that this adult is afraid of them. This staff member can also be the cause of anxiety for a child who fears that the nice, smiling, unresponsive adult cannot keep them safe.

When I would train new staff members, I had to tell them that the *screamer* and the *passive smiler* were both troubling to children. Both styles can make a youngster feel that they could be placed in danger at any time. That is why it is important for staff to set limits, abide by (fully explained) house rules, and, when necessary, administer logical consequences to children (covered in greater detail in chapter three). Staff members that respond inappropriately on either end of this spectrum risk failing the safety test.

Needs Met = Decreased Anxiety

To satisfy youths' needs it is sometimes necessary to fairly, appropriately and logically "consequence" them. Showing youngsters that staff cares enough to "deal with their behavior" (and the needs behind the overt actions) establishes safety for them and demonstrates that the staff member can maintain structure in the milieu, keeping the residents safe – no matter what.

It goes without saying that the staff member who *cares enough* to administer the consequence should bring closure to the issue. This can be done by discussing what led to the consequences. A good method for this can be adapted from the *life space interview* developed by Frizt Redl. This process reviews what happened, why it happened, and establishes an alternative (behavior) plan for the future. The example below will serve to shed light on this process:

> *A group of children in a residential placement setting have just watched a movie, and now it is time for Johnny Jones to go to bed. Upon being told by staff that it is bedtime, Johnny becomes aggressive towards another client (Tommy) as he walks by him. Things become chaotic as Tommy gets up to fight back. After a few moments, Tommy is calmed down.*

Utilizing and adaptation of the *life space interview*, the staff member and Johnny Jones would discuss:

1. What exactly happened? (aggression)
2. Why did it happen? (the movie triggered something, or, the child wanted to stay up later, etc.)
3. What is the resolution? (the child should read a book for the half hour proceeding bedtime – or any other calm activity. Another resolution could be that when a movie elicits a bad feeling, the child will tell staff that he/she needs to take some personal time in their bedroom. Remember, the resolution is to remedy why a particular behavior occurred.)

Obviously, if Johnny had harmed the other child, or furniture had been destroyed, other consequences (restriction, restitution) might be in order.

When the *child's need* to feel safe in the milieu has been satisfied a breath of decreased anxiety surfaces. Children become more comfortable in their environment when they perceive safety has been established. This is a time when the child is able to work on other issues "put on hold" until he/she feels safe enough in the residence. At this point the therapeutic relationship between staff and client has a chance to grow. Though there will be times when the road can become rocky again, negative behavior will be dealt with consistently and the relationship will continue to flourish. It is this adult-child connection that is all-important to a child's treatment in the milieu (Seita, et al. 1996).

THE IMPACT OF THE PHYSICAL ENVIRONMENT

The impact of a clean and orderly milieu cannot be underscored. As stated by Charlie Appelstein in *No Such Thing As a Bad Kid* (1998):
> A disorganized, messy setting intimates the following sentiments: *Things are out of place here, Life is unpredictable; We don't take pride in our possessions;* or even, *We don't care about you.* For troubled children, who require a high degree of structure, predictability and safety, such chaos is a behavioral hazard (pg 68).

Troubled children (who have underdeveloped internal structures) need intensive external structures to experience a sense of order, organization and safety (Appelstein, 1998). These youth need to live in an orderly home environment. If they came from chaotic, unstructured homes why would programs (who are being paid to treat these children) replicate such an environment? Nicely painted homes, furniture that is in good condition, and carpeting that is still padded and comfortable tell children that we care about them.

Even the smallest details count. Some residential facilities, even those with small budgets, go to great lengths to make sure all the dining room chairs match. This is important. Programs need to make the environment as warm and as inviting as possible. This sentiment is expressed in the words of John Seita, an individual who grew up in the child welfare system. In describing one of his placements, Seita (1996) acknowledges:
> *The home wasn't unfit for human habitation, but it certainly lacked any pretense of providing for privacy or respect for dignity. The dusty and worn-looking brick exterior of the building was crumbling. Large rectangular windows, six feet high and about three and a half feet wide, provided our vision to the outside world. The interior lacked any feeling of home or happiness. It was large and the floors were covered with yellowing linoleum and area rugs. It wasn't a home....it was food and shelter* (pg. 14).

The physical appearance of the milieu is very important. We don't ever want the children to feel that the home they are living in is just "shelter" and nothing else. Many of them were removed from places that provided them just "shelter." These children need to believe that they are worthy. In this sense a clean, tidy, and organized milieu helps them to feel good about themselves and adds to their potential to feel safe. A dirty, cluttered, unorganized environment might convey to the children that they are not valued and are unimportant.

While we strive to keep the residence in order, it is inevitable that destruction will occur from time to time. After all, we work with emotionally scarred children, so occasional holes in the walls and doors should be expected. However, staff members must fight the temptation to let the destructive child live amidst the devastation they have created. If so he or she will once again feel like the messy kid living a messy life (Appelstein, 1998). While it is not unrealistic to have the child help repair the damage that they have caused, staff may have to restore the environment themselves, and in this scenario, find another way to hold the child responsible for his or her actions (Appelstein, 1998). It should not be acceptable to allow damaged walls and doors to go un-repaired.

There are many ways that we can keep the environment looking neat and orderly. In addition to daily maintenance and cleaning, there are things we can do to create an aesthetically pleasing home. Some ideas include:

- A coat of fresh paint on the interior walls every few years.
- Artwork on the wall that is reflective of culture.
- Cheerful curtains and window treatments.
- A plant or two.
- Modern bedrooms (including room themes, such as wall colors/bedding/posters reflective of a child's favorite movie. This is especially true with younger children in care.)

A spruced up environment sends a message of safety and caring (Appelstein, 1998). In regards to the children's bedrooms, the decorum is very important. Reflecting on my experiences when my wife Laurie and I worked in a residential setting, we allowed the kids to dictate the decorum of their rooms. At one point our residence had bedrooms that incorporated an *Aladdin* theme, a *Power Rangers* theme, a *Dinosaur* theme, and, for an older child, a sports theme. The rooms were freshly painted with new bedding and posters that reflected the room's theme. The children loved their rooms and felt comfortable and safe in them. More importantly, it provided them with space that was their own.

Another point of advice is to let the child help in the process of decorating their bedroom. When I went to the hardware store to pick out the paint to makeover a child's room, I brought that particular child with me. He helped pick out the paint colors and thereby felt that he had a say in the way his bedroom was going to look. Anytime we can involve the children in an activity, we should do just that. These youngsters are used to others exerting power and control over them. Why not let them have a say in the decorum of their bedroom? After all, this is the room (environment) in which the child will spend a fair amount of their time. Make it special!

THE UNCONDITIONAL BELIEF OF ONE ADULT

Charles Appelstein (1994) states that all children need one adult to believe in them, no matter what. John Seita grew up in placement and went on to write about his experience. He insists that the belief of a staff member who worked with him helped immensely (Seita, et al. 1996). Youth in our programs depend on us to keep them safe, provide for their basic needs, and support them in the good and bad times. Many of us not only had family members that we could depend on, but we also had teachers, coaches, etc., for guidance. Children in residential placement deserve the same.

Personally, I will never forget a resource teacher of mine, Mel Benson. When I was attending middle school (in the eighth grade) my English teacher did not feel I was reaching my potential, so I was sent to Mrs. Benson's resource class twice a week for extra help. At first, I was resentful. Why wouldn't the school just let me wallow in the class? Being a "C" student was okay with me. And, besides, being in Mrs. Benson's resource room carried a stigma with it. It was only a class for kids who needed special help. I begrudgingly went to the resource room, figuring that at least the work would be easy, but I was in for an awakening. While Mrs. Benson and her assistant Mrs. McManus were the nicest teachers one could ever ask for, they expected their students to work hard. To help me, Mrs. Benson would find out about things I was interested in. She then found ways to incorporate them into my writing skills. Before I knew it, I was working more diligently than ever. English was quickly becoming my favorite subject.

After a quarter, I made some strides and received a C+ in my English class. That was not good enough for Mrs. Benson. She said, "James Harris I will not accept anything less than a "B" on your next report card." She even said that I was "just too smart to be getting anything lower than "A." Mrs. Benson encouraged my creativity and utilized my story writing as a way to help me with my grammar. She taught me to use my vast imagination and not hide it. She made writing fun.

By the time the next quarter ended, I was no longer underachieving. Mrs. Benson had installed a confidence in me that exists to this day. She taught me that if I applied myself, I could master anything. More than anything else, she dared me to dream. She taught me not to be complacent or accept mediocrity. I moved onto high school and mastered my English classes, moving up into college preparatory work. I attribute my progress to Mrs. Benson's belief in me.

The great thing about Mrs. Benson is that her life is a living example of the lessons she taught her students. She never let anything get her down and always believed in helping people. Later in life, she was touched by tragedy when her son and husband died. Mrs. Benson did not drift into an uneventful, untroubled retirement. Instead, she entered the political arena and became a member of Rhode Island's House of Representatives. There, Representative Benson has become known as a tenacious leader who always looks out for those that the system would rather forget. In fact, some of her peers in the House have told me they'd rather support her in a legislative endeavor than go against her.

Mrs. Benson believed in me. She believed in my academic potential. Because of her and the lessons she taught me, I have been able to accomplish a great many things. I have learned to be creative. I have learned to dream and not be tied down by conventional forces. I have learned to be a leader. Children in our care also need the belief of (at least) one adult. They need someone to tell them they can do better, they can dream, and they are worthy. If we can't instill this message in them who will?

The Chance to Promote Change

Being a direct care worker in a children's residential program is a challenge. It bears enormous responsibilities. No other member of the team spends as much time with the child, in or out of the milieu. For this reason the job of the direct care staff member is most important. These workers are generally on hand to encourage youths to learn when they are not motivated, to reward change as it occurs, and to discuss feelings when youths are ready (Krueger, 1988).

The milieu continues to be the environment where children spend the majority of their time in treatment. It continues to be the environment in which change is most likely to occur. In addition, it is the place where children begin to trust adults and have their needs met. That is why it must be the primary focus of our work. It is why milieu therapy continues to remain so important.

Our goal must be to help children actualize the following statement: "I see now that the years ahead of me can hold anything that I wish....the space in front of me is unimagined and formless, waiting for me to shape it." (Weltner, 1988).

The ability for staff to see the unlimited potential of each child in treatment is all-important. It is through the care that these staff members provide that children will languish or move forward. Our labor must not only be work that provides treatment for the symptom(s) that brought the youngster into care, but it must also instill hope in the child. Residential treatment must incorporate keeping the child safe as well as allowing him/her the opportunity to heal and grow.

There is no doubt that all members of the agency team have a chance to promote change in children's treatment. While direct care workers spend the most time with the child, and are thereby thought by many professionals to be core change agents in a child's life, the other members of the team are also of vital importance. The next chapter will give a succinct overview of each of the following professionals on the team:
- Direct Care Staff
- Residential Supervisors/Program Managers
- Clinicians

In addition to reviewing the roles of agency staff, the next chapter will also define the various types of residential placement facilities for children, from shelters to independent living programs. This review will be intended to explain the common terminology utilized in the field. There is no doubting that sometimes we get lost in the language of our field, using initials and abbreviations, assuming our peers and those outside the field comprehend this language. The next chapter will attempt to shed light on what we do and how we do it. In the process, it will serve to provide meanings to terms used throughout the remainder of this text.

CHAPTER TWO
Roles

"We realize that what we are accomplishing is a drop in the ocean. But if this drop were not in the ocean, it would be missed."

Mother Theresa

This chapter will focus on the roles of agency staff members, as well as the different types of residential placements that children reside in. (There will also be an initial concentration on agency communication.) This chapter will serve to define terminology utilized throughout the rest of this text. It is important to note that when *residential placement* is referred to in this work, it is intended to mean all placements that children reside in, away from their biological homes. Residential placement means foster homes, group homes, residential treatment, staff secure facilities, independent living, and supervised apartment programs.

LACK OF INTERNAL COMMUNICATION

One of the main challenges that residential placement agencies may encounter is internal communication. I know that I faced this issue when I worked for a residential placement agency. It is also a problem that is voiced time and time again when I talk with personnel from these agencies. The lines of communication are not always as open as they should be in our field.

There are numerous factors that attribute to poor communication within an agency. Some of these may include:
- Philosophical differences amongst staff members.
- Varying educational degrees of agency personnel.
- Established agency hierarchies.

Human nature dictates that there are bound to be differences in opinion whenever a group of people with different philosophies, levels of experience, and educational degrees work together. In children's residential placement agencies, like almost any other profession, this is often the case. Just in terms of education alone, we see a gap between workers. Most clinicians and executives hold a Masters degree or higher. Supervisors would be deemed to hold at least a Bachelors degree. Direct care staff members may not hold any degree.

In terms of salary it is no secret that the lower one is on the agency ladder, the lower the salary. While this is logical, it does not mandate that direct care workers are unimportant. In fact, the opposite is true. This is reflected in the following graphics:

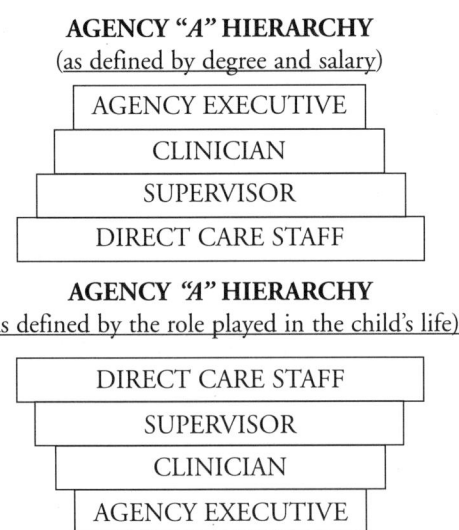

Obviously, the point of the first graphic shows that <u>the higher one moves up the ladder, the higher the salary and need for advanced degree</u>. The point of the second graphic is to show <u>that those workers having the most interaction with a child occupy higher rungs of this ladder.</u> In a nutshell, the higher one moves up the agency ladder, the further he/she moves away from the day-to-day treatment of youth. This is especially true in the larger agencies. However, this may not be the case in the smaller residential programs. In addition, clinicians at some programs may have as much interaction with the child as a supervisor.

We cannot prevent what happens within an agency hierarchy. We need our executive directors leading us, especially in this day and age. They have to be our voice in the public and our advocates before state and federal legislatures. Regarding clinicians, we know that they are important. They have the training and counseling skills necessary to provide treatment. Supervisors are just as critical, often balancing the needs of the agency as a whole. And, direct care staff members have the greatest chance to impact positive change in the life of a child in care.

While we acknowledge the need for an agency hierarchy and note the importance of each person's role, we must also acknowledge the vital importance of our day-to-day communication between members of the agency team. Verbal communication should never be allowed to break down. Children are placed within our programs for treatment. It is up to all members of the agency staff to make sure that they communicate. As the graphic below shows, the child should be the focal point of the team, with services being wrapped around him or her. This includes agency communication.

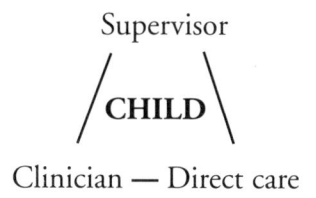

```
            Supervisor
             /      \
          / CHILD \
      Clinician — Direct care
```

If we do not have tight communication within the agency, the children suffer. In some instances we may even be replicating past patterns, where adults refusing to communicate have used youth as a pawn. That is why it is absolutely essential for team meetings to include all members of the agency team. It is one of the mantras of this text. For example, it is ill advised and at times unprofessional for an agency to conduct a consultation on a child without getting the input of all parties who work with him. Vital information could be ignored. More importantly, it is disrespectful of the needs of the children. It is a practice that breeds contempt amongst the agency team. It should never be occurring in this helping profession.

Denomination breeds division. We are all partners in the treatment of children in residential placement. In this field, where collaboration and networking is becoming a reality, why wouldn't this practice exist within our individual agencies? Good communication is essential for an agency to be successful in treating children. We all need to be on the same page.

ROLES WITHIN AN AGENCY

The next part of the chapter will focus on the three main roles within the residential placement setting: direct care workers, supervisors and clinicians. These roles were chosen for review only because they have the greatest connection to the milieu environment. It should be noted that this examination will look at personnel positions as they are designed in higher end residential placement agencies. For example, as the overview of residential programs will highlight, not all agencies have full time clinicians. Group homes, shelters, supervised apartment programs and foster homes may not. Another point to consider when reading this review is that I did not cover the role of foster parents. That is because this role is closely related (and highly applicable) to that of a direct care worker.

DIRECT CARE STAFF

We have all heard the latest *buzzwords* in our field: *accreditation, certification, managed care, performance measures and outcomes*, and, of course, *professionalism*. As we strive to find better ways to help children in residential placement, we are being asked to "produce better, more timely, and more cost effective results" with the youth in our charge. Thus, the importance of each discipline (role) on the agency team is seen as a vital part in meeting this new field mission.

Direct care staff members have the most interaction with children in residential placement. This means that they have the greatest potential impact in building relationships with youth in their care. Direct care workers are often responsible for the following (in no particular order):

- *Day-to-day basic care of the children.* This includes getting the children prepared for school in the morning, ensuring they get off to bed at a proper time in the evening, and everything else in between. Staff members must cook meals, keep the house tidy, help children maintain their hygiene, wash clothes, do the grocery shopping, etc.

- *Ensure the agency behavior management program is followed.* The next chapter covers this topic in greater detail. Basically, direct care staff must be well versed in administering the agency's behavior management program. These programs attempt to help children acquire more appropriate (socially acceptable) behaviors.

- *Provide compassion and emotional support to the children in their care.* Being an understanding person who can empathize with these youth is important.

- *Possess the ability to advocate for the children, and communicate the needs of the clients to the agency team.* Direct care staff members spend the most time with the children. Therefore they see many of the behaviors and can identify the needs. These workers must be able to communicate these needs to the various members of the agency team, especially the child's clinician.

- *Keeping up with paperwork demands.* This is an often overlooked aspect of the job. But the fact is that direct care workers are responsible for a lot of paperwork: daily logs, behavior management point system charts, filling out incident reports, signing medication sheets, etc.

- *The ability to not take things the children say personally.* This is another important (overlooked) part of the job. Direct care workers are going to be sworn at, kicked, spit at, and have their own family members called any number of names. Direct care staff members must use great restraint in these circumstances. The children will be waiting for these workers to "strike back" and validate their perception that all adults are bad.

- *Being a good role model.* This is the first and foremost duty of any direct care worker. Good role models are punctual, dress appropriately, do not swear at the children, nor do they become engaged in power struggles that end up with a child being physically restrained.

These are just some of the responsibilities and attributes for direct care staff members. In a snapshot these workers are parents, good listeners, tutors, landscapers, handy men and women, cooks, shoppers, transporters, disciplinarians, recreational planners, responsible advocates, problem solvers, and much more. They are vital to establishing a positive environment for children to reside in.

The creation of a residential environment that encourages growth, self-discipline and self-understanding is one of the major tasks of all those who work with children in care (University of Oklahoma, 1986). The direct care worker plays a key role in this occurring. Yet the difficulty of this undertaking can intimidate workers, leading them to focus on individual issues rather than the overall function of the residence (University of Oklahoma, 1986). This is why support systems must be established and in place for workers. Often these supports are provided as we move up the rung of the agency ladder. The next step of this ladder includes the supervisory position.

RESIDENTIAL SUPERVISORS/PROGRAM MANAGERS

Children's residential placement programs benefit from supervisory leadership that is well versed in the management of such facilities. This position presents many challenges as supervisors often bridge gaps between upper level administrators, direct care staff, and clinicians. Their effective leadership is essential to the employees that they supervise, and, more importantly to the children residing in these facilities.

I became a residential supervisor after five years as a direct care worker. I thought that I would simply waltz into my office (which was just a folding chair set up at a coffee table in the family visitation room) and help the program run as smoothly as ever. It didn't take long to realize that being a supervisor made me the buffer between warring parties, the spare to fill un-staffed shifts, the individual responsible for solving programmatic crises, and other issues for which I was not prepared. I thought I would just supervise staff and visit the kids in the milieu setting. Was I in for a rude awakening! The residential supervisor's job is not just a walk in the park.

Some of the tasks a residential supervisor is responsible for are:
- *Direct supervision of residential staff.* This task can never be overlooked or taken for granted. Residential supervisors should provide both individual supervision and group supervision, bringing the team together. Supervisors do not have an office only job. They need to be available for their staff. They should also be a visible presence in the milieu. This not only shows support for staff, but also conveys an agency's commitment and concern for the children.

- *Hiring and training direct care staff.* Another tough undertaking is hiring the right people to fill direct care positions. (In larger agencies this may be the task of a Human Resources Department.) When there are high turnover rates in these positions, the job is even tougher. It is sometimes tempting to hire anyone to alleviate the staffing shortage. This places the children in danger, so a good supervisor will continue looking for the right staff to work shifts at the house and keep the children safe.

  In addition, the supervisor must be able to train staff in the *basics*. This is especially true when they have hired a new worker. While outside training is a good way to show staff they are valued, the supervisor almost always does initial training. For this reason the supervisor must be well versed in the agency's behavior management, crisis intervention, and other programs.

- *Being an effective middle manager.* Being a residential supervisor can be a thankless job. The supervisor must maintain agency rules and regulations while being supportive of his or her staff. Residential supervisors must be able to advocate for staff while understanding the executive team's rationale for certain initiatives. Effective middle managers can understand the differing perspective of the professionals on a team while trying to find (and establish) that common ground.

- *Scheduling.* Creating a schedule may be one of the most taxing aspects of a supervisor's job. One must keep a multitude of things in mind when doing this: who needs what days off, what folks work well together, what is going on in the milieu during the week, and, what shifts am I (the supervisor) going to have to cover.

- *Promoting open communication and team building.* There is a line in a *Pink Floyd* song that states "All we have to do is make sure that we keep talking." Supervisors are often responsible for making sure this occurs. Clinicians and direct care staff have to talk. They have to find ways to help children collectively. It is not the supervisor's role to say to his/her staff, "The clinician said you must do this," or to state to the clinical team, "the direct care worker said this is how they are going to consequence a child no matter what you say." The supervisor is responsible for opening the lines of communication and holding team meetings where all parties come together to discuss the children.

It's back to communication skills, again. But the topic is so important it is worth another look. The last supervisory task to be covered in this section is the facilitation of *constructive confrontation*. This can be difficult. We work in a field whereby we tell children to talk about what's bothering them and to express their feelings appropriately with words. Yet, we do not always put these principles into practice as adults. There are endless cases of direct care staff (and clinicians) going to the residential supervisor with complaints about other direct care workers.

An important consideration in these cases is how the supervisor handles complaints brought to him/her. Does the supervisor listen? Does he/she let the staff member vent? These two practices are fine; however, the supervisor should be leery about confronting a staff member with complaints made by another. When I was confronted by such incidents as a supervisor, my response would be, "I hear your frustration and understand where you are coming from. Have you discussed this issue with_____?" If they would answer "no," I would direct them to do so. If the individual wouldn't confront his/her peer and continued to talk about that person I would set up a meeting between the two. I would sit in as a neutral party. This is sometimes the only way to get a grievance out into the open – and resolve it. While it isn't easy and it can be uncomfortable, the supervisor must make sure that staff members work together in a professional manner.

CLINICIANS

Clinicians are a vital part of any residential program. They play a major role in ensuring a child's treatment needs as well as a myriad of other tasks including visitation, court hearings, permanency planning, and making sure that the child's treatment plan is in accordance with the youth's needs. The list could go on and on....

In addition, as the field continues to change to a system that demands more timely results with children in residential placement, there is greater pressure on agencies (and clinicians) to ensure that youth are moved through the *continuum of care system* at a steady pace. Clinicians need to be in touch, on a consistent basis, with how the child is progressing in accordance to their treatment plan. Obviously, the child's progress in the residence is paramount in terms of importance. Some of the clinicians' tasks include:

- *Treatment plans, including permanency planning.* The child's success is often predicated by sound, concrete planning. In relationship to permanency, a plan for discharge (and how and when this will occur) should be established the day the child enters the program.

- *Case planning and reviews.* The clinician's job is so important because it always revolves around not only planning, but reviewing the progress a child is making in the program.

- *Therapy (individual, group and family).* This is often seen as the central (and vital) role of the clinician. It is within these sessions that clinicians utilize their expertise and education.

- *Training staff.* Clinicians have to train staff in key concepts as they relate to caring for children. Clinicians must be able to train in a manner that is respectful of the entire agency team. They must also be able to help staff whenever there is a question involving a treatment matter.

- *Educational endeavors.* Maintaining education is important. Clinicians must seek licensure, obtain Continuing Education Units and need to be aware of the latest in therapy models and practice.

- *Communication with direct care staff.* This has been covered throughout this chapter.

- *Visiting the child in the milieu.* Therapy within the clinical office is crucial. However, clinicians also need to visit the child in their milieu environment. Clinicians are the captains of the child's treatment team, so they need to know as much about the child's life as possible. Since the children spend a majority of their time in a residential setting, clinicians need to go out to the home periodically.

The clinician's role is the focal point in any child's treatment. This quick overview was intended to highlight only a fraction of this role. As was mentioned earlier, the clinician is critical in ensuring that the child is receiving proper treatment within all programmatic aspects. It is in relationship to this statement that direct care workers rely on the clinical team to assist them in helping the children in the milieu setting. In this light, the importance of the clinician's role in a child's treatment can never be underscored.

RESIDENTIAL PROGRAM TYPES

To most folks who do not work within the field there is a simplistic misconception about the work accomplished. They just assume children and youth who are removed from their families live in *group homes* or *foster homes*. In the earlier part of the 19th century, these children lived in *orphanages*. However, children's residential placement programs are much more than simply *group homes* or *foster homes*. This final section of the chapter will generically serve to note some of the different program types. They will be listed from a restrictive to least restrictive setting.

Sex Offender Treatment: This is specialized treatment in a highly secured setting. The amount of security can encompass the latest in electronic technology, including infrared lighting to detect a client movement, to video cameras in the hallways. Most youth in these settings are adolescent perpetrators who are at risk to harm others. On-site treatment includes residential, clinical and educational services. This intensive treatment is highly specialized and very costly. The problem our field is addressing is a *Catch-22* syndrome regarding sex offender clients. Some citizens do not want to pay the high costs to send youth to these programs, but they also don't want them on the streets. That is why we must have more sex offender step-down programs available to help the clients' transition to a less restrictive setting. We just can't keep adolescents locked in these settings until they are adults – and then expect them to go back into their communities and experience instant success.

Residential Treatment: This is the standard "high end" treatment for children and youth in out-of-home care. These agencies have their own clinical and educational programs in addition to the residential setting. Because these facilities have their own clinical departments and higher staff-child ratios in the milieu environment (sometimes one adult to every two children), the treatment is expensive. However, states rightly expect that these programs will render positive outcomes for the children placed there. The ages of youth in residential treatment facilities could run the range from 6 to 18.

Staff Secure: This type of placement is another form of a residential treatment program. Like the aforementioned, staff secure programs provide clinical and educational services in addition to intensive residential treatment. These programs are highly structured and serve to stabilize aggressive (mostly adolescent) youth. Staff secure programs either have "locked" facilities or the youth are physically prevented from leaving the premises.

Group Homes: The more traditional setting for children and youth is the group home. These programs provide residential care and some clinical services. Unlike the larger residential treatment facilities, there is apt to be one licensed therapist on staff who provides clinical services. Children residing in these programs would most likely attend public schools. Ages of youth in group homes would also be in the 6 to 18 range.

Shelters: These facilities are temporary placements. There are shelters for older adolescents as well as *kiddy* shelters (who even care for newborns). These are typically 45-90 day placements until the youth can move back home or into longer term residential care. (However, it is not uncommon for youth to remain in shelters for much longer than 90 days.) Like the group homes, shelters provide residential care and limited clinical services.

Independent Living: Independent living programs are designed for adolescents 16 years and older. There are two classes of programs: *supervised apartment* and *independent living* (typically for young adults 18 and older). These programs attempt to prepare clients for life "on their own." These young adults live in apartments, attend school and/or work a job. They are also monitored by a caseworker assigned to them by an agency. Staff supervision is greatly reduced, especially in the independent living programs for older clients.

Foster Homes: This is the least restrictive, least expensive type of residential placement. In most cases the youth (ages range from the very young until 18 or older) live with a family in the community. The family is (in many instances) supported by a parent agency with case management and clinical and consultative services provided. Sometimes counties retain their own roster of foster parents, and in many cases these individuals feel they do not have the proper supports and resources to assist them. Because of the low reimbursement rates and lack of supports, foster parents have become more and more difficult to recruit.

KEEPING EXPECTATIONS ABOUT OUR WORK IN CHECK

This chapter will close with a metaphor regarding residential care that I heard Charles Appelstein relate during a training in 2002 entitled *Residential Treatment From a Child's Perspective*. Charlie cited the need for residential workers to have appropriate expectations for the children in their care. He told the audience:

If you work at MacDonalds, you should expect to see hamburgers; and if you work in a setting with troubled, acting out kids you should expect to see.........acting-out! But, unfortunately, most workers have trouble with this analogy. A good night at MacDonalds is when a lot of hamburgers were sold, yet a good night at a residential facility usually means minimal to no acting out. And that's not always the case. A kid's best day in residential care could be the day that he had three tantrums after hearing some terrible news – but in each situation he was treated with respect and was able to meaningfully talk about his situation and learn new coping skills. Sure, our job is to help kids make better decisions and improve their behavior, but kids don't improve overnight. First, we need to hang in with them and establish trust. Rough nights will always be part of the package. Without them we don't get truly good ones.

The greatest chance to impact change in troubled children is when a youngster is having behavioral difficulties. This is when the team can come together and discern how to best help the youth. It is through teaching children better ways to deal with their feelings, through more socially acceptable behavior, that our work is accomplished. The next chapter will cover some behavior management techniques utilized in our field. In reviewing behavior management concepts, the reader will hopefully be alerted to the potential he/she has to help troubled youth in residential placement.

CHAPTER THREE
Behavior Management

"Children need models more than critics."
Joseph Joubert

Perhaps no other concept has as many definitions in our field as "behavior management." It means different things to different people. Its utilization within a residence can be proactive or punitive. Programs all have the same goal with children in their residences, but many employ differing styles of behavior management. What works for some doesn't work for others, and what some children respond to, others do not. Yet, in any viable training program, conference, or workshop, the issue of behavior management is never ignored. It can't be.

This chapter will focus on a practical approach to behavior management. It will consider the types of children with whom we work. The chapter will incorporate biological bases for an individual's behavior, theory, a review of some behavior management models, and an acknowledgement that each agency has a right to practice its "form" of behavior management. The real importance of an agency's behavior management program is that it must be taught in detail to the staff members responsible for carrying it out.

BIOLOGICAL BASIS OF BEHAVIOR

Most research agrees that our behavior is formed from experiences as well as our organic structure. For example, the human brain is responsible for many functions: memory, emotions, learning, and behavior. And this is just from the portion of the brain known as the limbic system. The brain, as with any part of human anatomy, is a complex organ that can be greatly influenced by the environmental system in which an individual lives.

We have known for some time now that environment plays a role in the psychopathology of individuals. In *Behavioral Neurology* (1992), Jonathan Pincus and Gary Tucker have given us research on the very subject by reflecting a thorough investigation of behavioral neurology. It is mentioned here as a book for those interested in learning more on the subject because it provides a good understanding of the limbic system, other portions of the brain, and how the brain is impacted by environment. Below is a diagram of the mid-line view of the brain and the region in which the limbic system is located.

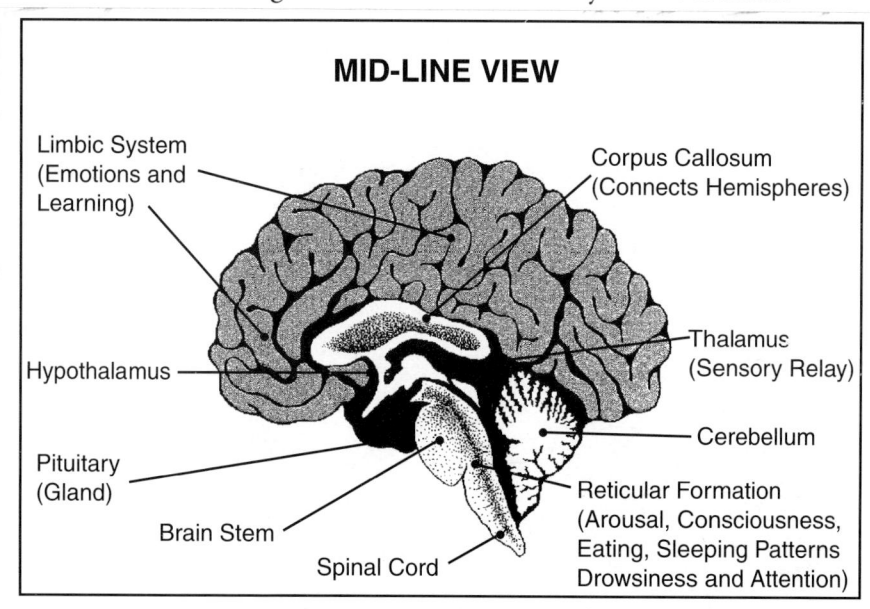

MID-LINE VIEW

- Limbic System (Emotions and Learning)
- Corpus Callosum (Connects Hemispheres)
- Hypothalamus
- Thalamus (Sensory Relay)
- Pituitary (Gland)
- Cerebellum
- Brain Stem
- Reticular Formation (Arousal, Consciousness, Eating, Sleeping Patterns Drowsiness and Attention)
- Spinal Cord

Many of the areas in the limbic system (sometimes thought to be more of a philosophical concept as opposed to a discrete anatomical or physiological system) are among the oldest portions in the cortex (Pincus & Tucker, 1992). Scientifically stated, the limbic system is the ring of gray matter and tracts bordering the hemispheres in the medial portion of the brain that play a role in human emotions (Pincus and Tucker, 1992). The three main structures (critical for human functioning) in the limbic system are the *olfactory system* (SENSORY system), the *amygdala* (the area responsible for FEAR), and the *hippocampus* (MEMORY).

The **olfactory system** begins at the roof of the nasal cavity. Its receptors are lined with cells that have additional receptors capable of detecting thousands of odors. This fragile tract is susceptible to shearing forces in head trauma, affecting the sense of smell.

The **amygdala** is responsible for the lurch in your stomach when you wake up in the middle of the night and see a shadow run past your bedroom window. It combines a learned sensory stimulus (an intruder approaching you = danger) to an adaptive response (fight or flight).

The **hippocampus** is involved in memory. While the olfactory system and amygdala are briefly highlighted, the hippocampus requires a broader explanation. There are three types of memory that are explained here:

The *sensory stage* calls attention to our memory process immediately after initial perception and/or information stimulation. This stage can be altered by image or sound. It is quick in deployment, lasting 1/100th of a second. The sensory stage serves as a directional for incoming and outgoing information being filtered (Tortora & Evans, 1990).

The *short-term memory* is where information is sorted and its destination determined. It processes information such as phone numbers and street addresses. Its duration lasts from fifteen to twenty seconds. Since short-term memory is fleeting, one must decide how important an item is, and in the case of a phone number, jot it down. Our minds would be far too cluttered if we relied on our memory to store phone numbers, addresses and birthdates.

The *long-term memory* is a permanent storage center. It is thought to have an unlimited capacity. Once information is settled in our long-term memory it usually stays there. The most difficult part of the informational journey to the long-term memory entrance is to get through the "bottle neck" that is known as short-term memory (Tortora & Evans, 1990). Any information that makes it to this final memory stage is very important to the individual.

This limited review of the three aforementioned structures of the limbic system serves only to show how important this structure is to the human brain. The encapsulated review also attempts to show how the limbic system is critical to human behavior. Studies in animals and humans have determined that the structures within the limbic system influence memory, learning, emotional states, visceral and endocrine responses, and behavior – particularly aggressive, oral and sexual activity (Pincus & Tucker, 1992). When one considers the relationship between the limbic system and emotions, learning, and memory, it can be predicted that diseases (and damage) involving limbic components could cause emotional disorders.

THE IMPACT OF ABUSE AND NEGLECT ON THE BRAIN

The brain is a bottom-up organization with the bottom regions (brainstem and midbrain) controlling the simplest functions, such as respiration, heart rate, and blood pressure regulation (Perry, 2002). The top areas (limbic system and cortex) control more complex functions, such as thinking and regulation of our emotions (Perry, 2002). The development of the brain is sequential. This means that the bottom portions of the brain develop first, followed by the top. The consequence of sequential development is that as different regions of the brain are organizing, they require specific types of experiences targeted towards the region's specific function (i.e., visual input while the visual system is organizing) in order to develop normally (Perry, 2002).

Unfortunately, while some youth are experiencing healthy childhood development, others are in the throes of abuse and neglect. This can have a profound impact on the developing brain. During traumatic experiences, these children's brains are in fear-related activation, stimulating key neural systems in the brain which lead to adaptive changes in emotional, behavioral and cognitive functioning to promote survival (Perry, 2002). This can lead to a persistent fear-state in children who have been abused and neglected. This fear response can result in children becoming hypervigilant, anxious, and behaviorally impulsive and lead to the development of physical signs, such as attentional, sleep, and mood problems (Perry, 2002). Residential facilities treat many of these children.

To further relate how biological bases of behavior impact children in care, Pincus and Tucker (1992) relate a study of adjudicated adolescent males in the 1980's. Though the research is nearly twenty years old, it is still interesting. The study consisted of 97 juvenile offenders. Each subject was examined by a neurologist and psychiatrist. Psychological tests and EEGs were performed. The findings concluded that:

In the more violent group, 81% had either minor and major neurological signs (disturbances). Virtually all of the subjects came from the lower echelons of society, and most were from broken homes with multiple social problems, including criminality, alcoholism, and mental illness in parents (p.81).

Studies such as this confirm how the environment can negatively impact biology. Its inclusion in this text serves to show the correlation between whence our children came, how they were impacted, and how their behavior has been shaped. This charges us with the task of developing behavior management programs that help youth develop more socially acceptable behavior. In doing this we must recognize that there is a particular catalyst to each and every overt behavior.

The aforementioned study demonstrates how the environment and one's learning influences one's behavior. In children's residential placement facilities, we see a number of youth who have come from broken homes, settings that could be chaotic and in the hands of adults with drinking and/or other problems. These children may come into residential programs with numerous issues and suffer from low self-esteem. They can be highly aggressive and may have acquired many maladaptive behaviors as a result of their environment. Some of these behaviors might include hoarding food (they may have not been fed adequately), intimidating peers (they may have seen how the threat of violence can be rewarding), and poor hygiene skills.

Meeting Needs

There is a principle that states *people act in specific ways to have their needs met.* It is not a premise to be debated. Just as we accept that there is a biological base for human behavior, we must also accept that human beings endeavor to have their needs met. It is an important fact that we must remember when we work with the children in our care to help us remember their plight. If only one thing is taken from this text, remember that everyday we strive (either consciously or unconsciously) to have our needs met. This is an important concept in our work with children in residential placement.

Abraham Maslow (1908 – 1970) was one of the founders of humanistic psychology and his work still makes perfect sense today. Maslow is famous for his needs hypothesis, which is still utilized widely today by a multitude of professions. His book, *Motivation and Personality* (1985, third printing) is an exploration of personality development through humanistic principles. He regarded human needs set up like a ladder. The most basic needs were at the lower rung. The diagram below details Maslow's **Hierarchy of Needs:**

SELF-FULFILLMENT
PSYCHOLOGICAL (ESTEEM)
SOCIAL (BELONGING) (LOVE)
SECURITY (SAFETY)
PHSYIOLOGICAL (SURVIVAL)

The most basic of all needs are found on the lower level. The individual's movement up the hierarchy occurs when he/she is motivated by a higher need - and the lower need has been satisfied. Maslow's work is developmental in nature. It applies to the children we care for in residential treatment because they may not be accustomed to having their needs met. Looking at each stage more closely will bring this fact into the light.

Physiological (Survival) Needs. These are the basic needs of survival: food, shelter, water, etc. Humans, like other animal organisms, have a strong drive towards self-preservation. Many children now residing in out-of-home placement may not have had all of their survival needs met. It is not unexpected that it will take these children time before they are feeling secure.

Security (Safety) Needs. There are two types of security needs of primary importance: physical and emotional. Focusing on our work with children, it is easy to discern that some physical needs may not have been nurtured to. Were healthy relationships developed? Were the children safely cared for by adults who openly showed them love and compassion? Or, did they have to worry about their safety on a daily basis? The same questions can be asked regarding their emotional needs.

Social (Belonging) Needs. In addition to security, we need social belonging. We want to feel accepted. We need to feel that we belong. For many children in care this need is sorely lacking. Unless we work hard at it, it is easy for children in care to feel a disconnection from other members of the milieu, their peers, and their family.

Psychological (Esteem) Needs. In varying degrees we all seek recognition and prestige. We all want to be noted and put up on a pedestal even if only for a moment or two. Children in care are no different. That is why we must take every opportunity to recognize even the smallest victory in anything they accomplish. Children need to be thought well of by others, as well as themselves.

Self Fulfillment Needs. These are the highest of all needs as we progress toward optimal potential. They are also referred to as our self-actualization needs. They rank as the ultimate goal of all individuals. It is the end result of our hope for youth in care: *we want to help our children recover from the trauma of their past so they can envision a brighter tomorrow – and they can become productive members of our society.*

Maslow believed that once a need is satisfied (or nearly satisfied) it lessens in severity as a strong motivator. Rarely is a need completely satisfied, nor does it ever completely stop to be a motivator. However, it does lose some of its command. For example, if a child receives a cone of ice cream each time he/she completes his or her homework without any mistakes, an attempt to further motivate with extra ice cream might not be as effective as other actions.

Our difficult task is to translate what we know about needs into action that meets the needs of children in care. No two people are the same. All children's needs vary in type and intensity. The premise of Maslow's theory is that human behavior is a result of various attempts to meet some unmet need. When residential staff members are attempting to meet the needs of a child it should be remembered that:

1. When there is a conflict between lower-level and higher-level needs the lower-level needs will be acted upon. (A child who is hungry will be more interested in securing food than participating in a group exercise).

2. Individuals constantly seek to move up the hierarchy.

3. An individual's needs are ongoing and changing. We are always striving to satisfy a need at some level.

4. Depriving a child of need fulfillment by a worker will generate behavioral responses from the child.

Maslow's theory is one of hope for the individual. Humanistic psychology as a whole gave rise to several different therapies. All of these treatment models are guided by the idea that people possess the inner resources for growth and healing. The models also suggest that if people's natural inclination toward positive growth is slowed down or stopped, it is due to some "obstacle" in the pathway. Most helpers' main task is to help remove these obstacles. That is why workers must define a child's need and how best to help them meet the need. In this light, a child's behavior is presented as a way to assist in having his/her needs met.

VERBAL INTERVENTIONS UTILIZED IN BEHAVIOR MANAGEMENT

We want to help children in our care meet their needs, resolve unmet needs, and remove roadblocks. Most importantly, we must find a way to help youth extinguish maladaptive behavior. One way to accomplish this is through a multitude of verbal interventions. These cues should be seen as a way to redirect a child. Verbal interventions should be our first attempt in extinguishing inappropriate behavior. These interventions do not require yelling, screaming, and can be very effective prompts.

Verbal interventions show empathy and concern for the youngster. They also convey the adult's understanding of where the youth is "coming from." The first model (amongst many that can be reviewed) is commonly called **supportive statements.** They are meant to comfort a child during a time of emotional unrest (Appelstein, 1998). Examples of such statements are as simple as: "Oh boy, Bobby, you must really be angry" or "Sally, you must feel terrible."

Another verbal intervention that works with a child is **positive feedback.** There is no doubting that many children in care may not be used to receiving praise. That is why when I was a direct care worker I always liked to give a child positive feedback whenever I had the opportunity. This was done no matter how small the accomplishment. An example would be "Wow, Justin, the way you placed tinsel on the Christmas tree was absolutely perfect. It looks just like the trees we see on Christmas shows on t.v." While I was *pouring it on*, we should never miss the opportunity to praise a child in our care. It meets a definite need.

There is something important to remember when praising a child. That is, we should praise the act – not the child. We want to respond to the behavior, not the child as a person (Whitman, 1991). (Example: "Great job making that sandwich, Sally." We wouldn't say, "Good girl.") Words should be short, clear, and to the point. The tone should also be reflective of the praise being given to a child. Children know when staff members are laboring to be positive. Be genuine.

There is also the need for a **logical verbal reaction,** especially if a behavior warrants a consequence. An example of this is in relating a story of a youngster I once worked with named Michael. One night he and I were watching a Super Bowl game. He was so upset when his team began to lose. I tried to redirect him when he began to swear under his breath. Later when he began to punch the floor, I tried to redirect his behavior again. Finally he stood up, grabbed his beanbag chair, and threw it across the room at the television. I had to tell him, "Mike, you need to take a time out in your room. What you just did makes me feel very uncomfortable. If all the kids were allowed to throw things around the living room it wouldn't be very safe around here." Such statements explain to the child that he or she is being consequenced because his or her behavior carries serious implications.

As we continue to explore verbal interventions, it should be noted that the aforementioned strategies are not new theoretical concepts. People may label them in different terminology. Two additional responses that I like come from Charles Appelstein (1998). They are **connecting statements** and **explorative responses.**

Connecting statements occur when the staff and child are on different sides of an issue. With this verbal intervention the staff member takes a step back to make a connecting statement (Appelstein, 1998). Such an example is, "You know, I don't enjoy the fact that we disagree. You and I are on the same side. We all want you to be happy here. The tension here stinks." Connecting statements can be commonly practiced, especially in limit setting situations. Personally, I would always try to use a statement as noted in the example. It showed that I really wanted to help the child. Connecting statements help reduce staff power (a big issue for children in care) and, in general, helps to diffuse tension (Appelstein, 1998).

The **explorative response** is also highly effective. We have all experienced numerous situations where we just know that a behavior is masking an underlying pain. At times it is appropriate to explore the possible source(s) of the symptomology in a manner such as, "You know I have never seen you react like this over something so small. Is anything else bothering you?" This type of response is effective. The only drawback with this is that some programs still believe that discussions about a child's family and/or other psychological material should only be conducted between the child and his/her therapist. This might result in the child being asked to stop talking and wait until Monday morning to speak to his/her therapist (when he or she is ready to talk on Friday night).

In the ideal milieu, all staff (direct care included) are trained in the therapeutic dynamics and verbal interventions and are ready to talk when the (rare) opportunity arises. Children in residential care are often defensive and unwilling to *open up*; they generally don't trust adults. When a child begins to honestly express his fears, emotions, and confusion, it's like a door opening up and the immediate task of the staff member – whoever it is – is to jam his or her foot in that door and engage the child (Appelstein, 2002, personal conversation). Two days later when he/she attends therapy, the child will probably have difficulty returning to the evocative subject matter that surfaced prior to the weekend. And that's a missed opportunity.

Direct care workers should be trained to talk with children when the situation arises, but they can also be encouraged to make such comments as, "This seems like an important talk. Can I relay what we're discussing to your therapist?" Of course, if a worker is new or doesn't feel comfortable talking with a child about certain subjects, the staff member could tell the child that he/she will find someone more experienced at handling such conversations.

LOGICAL CONSEQUENCES

It would be a perfect world if all we had to do as staff members was administer verbal interventions and the children would respond. This would rectify the behavior and the child's needs would be met. But if that were the case the youngster(s) would not be with us in the first place. Our jobs are to help hurting kids. Often that means taking the next step. When verbal interventions are not working we must go to logical consequences. This is the next practical step.

Rudolph Dreikurs (1897-1972) is widely accepted to be the father of logical consequences. Dreikurs believed that 90% of a child's behavior is for attention (Wichman, 2002). As discussed in this chapter, it is part of our work to determine what a child's behavior is telling us and to help children develop more appropriate ways to express their feelings. Therefore, decisions regarding discipline must remain logical and pro-active. This was a major theme in Dreikurs' work. Though much of his theory was developed to apply to classroom settings, his work can be carried over to our profession. The *Education Development* (2002) study highlights some of Dreikurs' recommendations. They include:

- Give clear-cut directions for the actions expected of each child.
- Try to establish a relationship with each child, based on trust and respect.
- Let children assume greater responsibility for their own behavior.
- Combine kindness and firmness. The student must always sense the adult is a friend, but that this adult would not accept certain kinds of behavior.
- At all times distinguish between the deed and the doer. This permits respect for the child, even when they do something wrong.
- Set limits from the beginning, but work toward mutual understanding, a sense of responsibility, and a consideration for others.
- Close an incident quickly and revive good spirits. Let children see that mistakes are corrected, and then forgotten.

This list provides a good example of ways to set rules and limits while respecting the children. The recommendations are not punitive and actually serve to bolster a child's self-esteem. Dreikurs' believed that professionals should use logical consequences as opposed to traditional punishment, with the consequence bearing a direct relationship to the behavior and must be understood by the child (Wichman, 2002).

A logical consequence is just that. There is no better term for it. In fact, the more out of control kids appear, the more *appropriately* controlling we must be to help restore their sense of safety and well-being (Appelstein, 1998). These consequences require that we put aside our frustration with the behavior in order to discern a consequence that is logical. An illogical consequence and then a logical one will follow the scenario on page 43:

> *Paul is a seventeen-year-old who is in his room one rainy afternoon listening to the latest Eminem CD. Staff has asked him to use his head-phones as the language is not appropriate for some of the other children in the milieu. Paul is given verbal cues to turn it down. He refuses to cooperate. Instead, he turns the volume up even louder.*

<u>Illogical and Inappropriate Consequence</u>: Staff walks into Paul's room and announces, "Paul we tried to warn you but you didn't listen. You know that Red Sox game that we are going to on Sunday? (Paul is a big Sox fan.) Well, you're not going. And, if you don't turn the CD off now, you'll be going to bed early for the next week."

Obviously, the aforementioned consequence has nothing to do with the behavior.

<u>Logical Consequence</u>: Paul's CD player is taken away for the remainder of the day (or perhaps even the weekend if the behavior occurred on a Friday afternoon). This is more appropriate (logical) as the consequence is in direct response to the behavior.

Direct care staff members must make sure that the consequences they administer are logical, and not punishment. Punishment is not the answer. Punishment, in response to a behavior, can be construed as inappropriate adult power and control. It can be perceived as being used to bring about displeasure (pain) to a youth. Punishment assumes that psychological and physical pain will reduce undesirable behavior patterns (Krueger, 1988). Remember, the children in our care are used to such tactics from adults. They have experienced inappropriate discipline. If punishment (psychological and physical pain) worked in extinguishing negative behavior, our youth would be amongst the healthiest in the world (Krueger, 1988).

This section of the chapter is not intended to convey the message that verbal interventions and logical consequences will be the cure all in stopping deviant behavior. The point here is that if one can utilize these practices successfully it is more effective and proactive in one's work with children. Kids do not enter care to be disciplined. They are with us for treatment. It can sometimes be hard to remember that in our jobs.

Additional Examples of (Potential) Logical/Natural Consequences

BEHAVIOR OBSERVED   LOGICAL CONSEQUENCE

Will not eat meals — Today, most residential programs offer the child a substitute if he/she does not like the meal being served. This could be a peanut butter and jelly sandwich and some carrot sticks, etc. This is much more fair than (punitively) trying to force a child to eat something he/she does not like.

Bedwetting — <u>This can be more symptomatic than just a maladaptive behavior.</u> Keep things logical. Before school the child has to launder their bedding and put it in the dryer. After school he/she has to make the bed before going outside to play.

"Tattles" — Deal only with the behaviors you actually observe (consequencing a child based on a peer's accusation is not good practice). First, give the tattler and the accused the opportunity to work things out. Bring them together. If this doesn't work, it might be wise to separate them for a defined period of time. Children should also be taught the distinction between telling when a peer does something very serious versus a low level behavior. We want children to come forward when safety is being threatened.

(continued next page)

| *Splits Staff* | This is so common it is predictable. One might alert the youth that, *If this doesn't stop future decisions will only be made if both staff members talk and agree. This means if you want to go to the movies with another residence, and my partner isn't here to discuss it with me, you might not be able to go.* |

PHYSICAL INTERVENTIONS

In no instance is it acceptable for children to be physically consequenced for a behavior (i.e.: doing push ups and sit ups, etc.). In addition, there has also been a scrutiny of the way children are physically restrained in this country. For example, in my home state of Rhode Island, the legislature passed the *Child's Freedom From Restraint Act* in 1999. The act provides mandates for when a child can be physically held, and what crisis intervention models are acceptable. The legislature passed the bill overwhelmingly.

Nationwide there has been a close examination of crisis intervention practices within children's residential programs. It may be long overdue. The movement was set about in Congressional ranks after a series of articles in the *Hartford Courant,* describing child fatalities from physical restraint(s). Now limitations are being set on when/how a staff member can physically respond to a child. Too many youth were being hurt or killed in this country due to improper and unnecessary physical restraints.

Reviewing the Rhode Island policy, children's residential programs must have a certified trainer on staff in a nationally recognized crisis intervention model. All staff members must receive such training. Recertification is also mandated and not just for the trainer. This is the best part of the mandate. It guarantees that direct care staff members receive an appropriate amount of training. If a child is hurt during a restraint, there are penalties involved. Litigation can be initiated against the staff member, or against the agency itself if it did not provide the appropriate training.

While there were anxious moments for residential facilities in Rhode Island as the regulations were developed, the mandates should not be the deterrent to inappropriate physical restraint. Rather, the deterrent should be staff's response to the needs of the child that prevents such occurrences. Too many times restraints happen when a youth is verbally assaultive, disrespectful, or challenging a staff member. Sometimes it is just easier to *put a child down* then it is to deal with the symptom behind the overt behavior. A child should be restrained only if he/she is a danger to himself/herself or others.

This text does not proclaim to be an authority on the physical management of children in care. (The Appendix lists some crisis intervention programs.) It is up to each agency to decide which crisis intervention model it practices. In addition, it is up to the staff member to make sure that physical restraints are conducted only after other options have been exhausted. These restraints should never be introduced as a means of adult power and control. The better a staff member becomes with verbal interventions, he/she will find that physical interventions become more and more remote.

Questioning Your Behavior Management Program

An agency's behavior management model will depend on the program type and the population served. While it is the agency's responsibility to design its behavior management program, it is the staff member's obligation to question any components that are confusing or contradict the program's values. We deal with traumatized youngsters who benefit from a team effort that puts the needs of the children first. Agencies must discuss which behavior management strategies work best with the children in their care.

What works today with children in care may not work tomorrow. That is why behavior management approaches and techniques may need refinement. Perhaps the most important part in establishing and maintaining a behavior management program is keeping the needs of the youth we serve in focus. With this philosophy we can be assured that we are putting our best foot forward. We must accept the fact that a child's presenting behavior is a key factor in our being able to help him/her.

To summarize this very brief overview of behavior management, it is apparent that there are right and wrong ways in dealing with children, thus we have to take into account many things in our work. As presented in this chapter, some of the things we must ask ourselves when dealing with a child's behavior include:

- What need is the child attempting to have met through his/her behavior?
- What verbal interventions might work in a given situation?
- What consequence is logical, and appropriate, for a child's behavior?
- Is a physical intervention really necessary at this time?
- How can staff use this opportunity to teach the child to make better choices when he/she is in a similar situation?

If staff members can answer these questions they may have a better grasp on what a child's behavior is telling them.

CHAPTER FOUR
Human Stage Development

"Keep yourself clean and bright; you are the window through which you see the world."

George Bernard Shaw

Human development has always been a topic of immense interest to psychologists. It is obvious that stage development is useful to view how and why humans grow the way that they do. However, as we have now embarked on the 21st century, developmental psychologists have the potential task of "updating" this theory. They must look at how the human life span is altered by our "new world." Between omissions in past developmental theories and the changing world in which we live, the field must develop applicable suppositions for today's American society.

THREE TEXTBOOK VIEWS BRING US TO THE PRESENT DAY

In *The Developing Person Through the Life Span,* by Kathleen Berger (1994), the author states: "The study of human development is the study of how and why people change over time, and how and why they remain the same" (p.32). Berger (1994) gives a complete overview of human development and a great deal of her text is focused on earlier stages, from conception through adolescence. Her book focuses on both physiological and psychological growth. She reviews societal factors that influence human development. Her coverage of the formative years and how adolescent growth is influenced by our society is quite comprehensive.

Assembling a different focus is *Adult Life,* by Judith Stevens-Long and Michael Commons (1992). The authors of this text focus on the importance of studying adult development. They assert that adulthood, which spans the greatest amount of time in stage development, presents somewhat of a challenge for developmental psychologists to define. They believe that "researchers have to find a reasonable way to divide up the adult years in order to make the comparison that would tell us whether development occurs and how it proceeds" (Stevens-Long and Commons, 1992, p.23).

In *The Hurried Child*, by David Elkind (2001), the noted author looks at how parental roles and societal factors push children along, regardless of the individual's developmental pace. Elkind contends that hurrying children along can alter their developmental growth. This in turn burdens the child even as he/she enters adulthood. He implies that in this fast-paced society, we assume children are *super kids* who can keep up with the pace we project unto them. Elkind sarcastically states, "Like Superman, Super kid has spectacular powers and precocious competence even as an infant. This allows us to think we can hurry the little powerhouses with impunity" (p.xii).

The aforementioned texts focus on different areas of stage development, yet they all share a common principle - society impacts human development. This is common knowledge. The problem is that society can be viewed as playing a major role in negatively influencing stage development and we seem to be powerless in countering this. The challenge for developmental psychologists is to determine what can be done to rectify this problem. It is a juggling act at best. We must keep in mind political factors, cultural norms and modern day beliefs and practices.

Stage development has not always encompassed adulthood in its entirety. One could state that stage development has neglected to fully identify the societal impact(s) on human development. Many theories need to be modified to accommodate today's society. Therefore, we need to make decisions about what we think is best for the population(s) we serve. Can we take an eclectic approach and utilize pre-existing theories? Do we break new ground? Or, can one theory be "modernized" to fit today's concept of human development?

Erikson Still Makes Sense

It is the assumption of many (including this author) that the work of Erik Erikson can be utilized to study's today's complex life span. Erikson contrasts Freud's work in stage development in that he focused on psychosocial development (as opposed to Freud's psychosexual development). He looked at the development of the healthy personality while Freud focused on neurotic personality development. These two refinements to Freud's work have earned Erikson a great deal of respect in the eyes of developmental psychologists.

Erikson's stage development seems to be easier to relate to because it is comprehensive in nature. Many see the value of his work as it includes each stage of the life span. Erikson's *eight stages of man* cover birth through adolescence in detail. His work also makes in-depth overtures towards adult development. His three adult stages coincide with the three adult stages that Stevens-Long and Commons (1992) break down as early, middle and late stages of adulthood. Others see the benefit of Erikson's work in the area of social development. His stages focus on the individual's relationship with the social environment.

At the core of Erikson's theory was a certain crisis unique to each particular stage. This *turning point* was the key to each stage. If the individual resolved the crisis, they would move on to the next stage. If they could not resolve it, they would linger in this stage until they were able to do so. In the field of children's residential work, we see children stuck in the early stages of development. Even something as early as stage one, *Trust versus Mistrust,* whereby children are dependent on their parents, we see youth in our program who have not resolved the fundamental crisis of hope. Since they have not always been nurtured and cared for, some are not capable of trusting their caregivers.

Another example of Erikson's stage development, one that is complex and dealt with in many texts is stage five, *Identity Versus Role Confusion,* ages 12-18. The trying on of "different hats" by adolescents is very important. Adolescents try to figure out "Who am I?" It helps them narrow down who they are and who they will become. They establish sexual, political and career identities or are confused about what roles they play (Berger, 1994). This is a very trying stage. That is why in residential programs, especially if adolescents are kept in rigid routines (where structure is valued more that experiential learning), clients could experience great difficulty in resolving this stage.

Elkind (2001) acknowledges that in this time of inner searching, adolescents should not be rushed. They need to find themselves. If they are given the proper support from parents, guardians, peers and society the crisis can be resolved. Elkind (2001) contends:

> *Young people who have a consistent sense of their sex role, their success as students, their work habits, and their relations to adults and to their peer group, find that structuring a personal identity is a challenging and rewarding task* (p. 118).

Stevens-Long and Commons (1992) also support this stage as being one of the most important in the entire life span, insisting that in many instances adolescents enter young adulthood still trying to resolve the *Identity Versus Role Confusion* stage: Stevens-Long and Commons (1992) state that "The abilities and concerns expressed in adolescence – the search for personal identity, and independence – continue to be refined and consolidated throughout the early years of adult life. (p.96)

The support of Erikson's work is evident in all three of the aforementioned texts. Though each may define different areas, all concur that the psychosocial aspects of human development are most important. Human development is contingent upon how we adapt to our environment.

The New American Culture

Whether we are able to adapt to cultural influence is measured by the extent of adaptation that is required. Today, in American culture, especially after 9-11, things can seem to be out-of-hand and overwhelming. Berger (1994) warns that "Central to Erikson's theory, problems arise when a society's traditional methods of upbringing no longer prepare its children to cope with the demands they face as adults." (p.42)

Psychosocial theory is still extremely valid and beneficial to our *new world*. We have to look at the problems today's culture is presenting for our children. What can we do to help children grow in a society that seems to have forces that impede their development? Violence is more prevalent, drugs have become available to children at a younger age, and the nuclear family has rapidly become a thing of the past. We may not be able to change the world, but youngsters still need our help as they attempt to adapt.

Elkind (2001) had made it clear that we are a society moving at breakneck speed. We seem to look for ways to rush the growth of progress. As a result we push aside anything or anyone that moves too slowly. It is obvious what pushing kids along or aside does. It leaves the child vulnerable to all kinds of potential victimization (alcohol, drugs, criminal activity, teenage pregnancy, etc.). These are almost accepted givens in today's society. Elkind (2001) adds:

Only in the context of a society that is hell-bent on doing things more quickly and better, and is impatient with waiting and inefficiency, can we really understand the phenomenon of hurried children and hope to help them. (p.186)

Elkind's (2001) words echo loud and clear in our culture!

One could state that as a society we need to re-evaluate where we are heading. Times have always presented new problems for people to resolve, but never has violence and immorality seem to run so rampant in our country – and world. The time has come for us to stop, look, listen, and respond. Our field is left with trying to help the children of a country that prides itself on being the greatest society in the world. We know that there are many contradictions in this sentiment—just look at the youth we care for.

Psychologists in the next few decades must find better ways to help support families, individuals, and communities which are put under enormous stress by the complexities of this modern life (Kegan, 1996). While the world deals with the problems it has created, we in children's residential placement programs are left with the challenge of helping wounded youngsters. More than ever, we need to help the children in our charge graduate and progress through healthy stage development. We should utilize the work of theorists (like Erikson) to help us with these tasks.

ERIKSON'S EIGHT STAGES

STAGE ONE: *Trust Versus Mistrust.* (newborn to 18 months) Babies learn to trust those caring for their basic needs (nourishment, warmth, physical contact). If these needs are met the infant builds a sense of trust. If unmet, the child could develop a lack of confidence in others' providing care.

STAGE TWO: *Autonomy Versus Shame and Doubt.* (1-3 years). Children learn to do things by themselves (feeding, toileting, walking, talking). The parents' role is important, providing the child with praise and encouragement. Adults must give the child a good image of himself/herself.

STAGE THREE: *Initiative Versus Guilt.* (1-4 years). Children become creative and want to take part in more "adult-like" activities, sometimes pushing the limits set by a parent. Thus, feelings of guilt can occur. Adults should make children feel worthy, answer all their questions, and not simply brush them aside.

STAGE FOUR: *Industry Versus Inferiority.* (6-12 years). Teachers and peers become important in this stage as children learn to master new skills. Teachers and other adults should help the child be successful and recognize accomplishments. Children will either feel competent or believe they cannot do anything right.

STAGE FIVE: *Identity Versus Role Confusion.* (12-20 years). Adolescents try to discern who they are, and what roles they play in life. They discover their political, sexual and career identities or they can become uncertain regarding their self-roles/worth.

STAGE SIX: *Intimacy Versus Isolation.* (Young Adulthood). Individuals seek companionship and relationship with another person. Jobs and careers are important as well as setting goals. The individuals learn to love and commit to relationships or can become isolated fearing rejection and/or disappointment.

STAGE SEVEN: *Generativity Versus Stagnation* (Middle Adulthood). Individuals "give" to the next generation through their meaningful work/creation. They rear families and develop a sense of community or they can become self-absorbed, uncaring and selfish.

STAGE EIGHT: *Integrity Versus Despair.* (Older Adulthood). Individuals look back on their life, assessing its worthiness. They gain wisdom and an acceptance of how their life was lived or they despair at goals never reached and questions that remain unanswered.

Erikson believed crises could be resolved in later stages but that it would be more difficult. In our work with children in care, this is usually the case, especially in the first three stages. Many youth in residential placement did not receive the proper care as infants. They did not receive praise and encouragement. Many did not have the good fortune of being able to overstep limits without facing dire consequences from adults. It is evident when working with these youth that they have many crises to resolve. It is our responsibility to help them.

In this book (in the chapters on milieu therapy and behavior management) there is much discussion on helping children meet their needs. This premise is a good context for Erikson's stages as they relate to the children that we serve. When we see a ten-year-old child we cannot automatically assume that he/she will be ready to learn (and master) new skills and be creative. He/she could very well be stuck in an earlier stage. It is not uncommon for many of our children to fear adults. That is why meeting the child's needs is important. It assists in healthy growth. The chart below gives examples of how to help a child (meeting needs) that may be stuck in stages 1-3 (as defined by Erikson):

STAGE	PROBLEM	HOW NEED CAN BE MET
1: Trust Versus Mistrust	Hordes food	Basic needs evident: food, clean room, safety. Do not withhold food – ever.
2: Autonomy Versus Shame and Doubt	Bathroom issues, cannot use utensils during dinner	Build self confidence, praise child for minor/all accomplishments
3: Initiative Versus Guilt	Shies from group activities, inward self focus	Child-adult conversations, answer all questions; make child feel worthy.

The aforementioned chart is an example only. You can, and should, find other examples for each stage as it applies to the children in your care. The chart was intended to give brief examples as to the value of Erikson's work even today – and how it can be utilized within our field.

Cognitive Theory – Piaget

Jean Piaget (1896-1980) is the most famous of cognitive theorists. He first became interested in thought processes while field-testing questions being considered for a standard intelligence test for children (Berger, 1994). He was supposed to find the age at which children could answer each question. However, he became more interested in their wrong answers. He noticed that children who were the same age made similar mistakes in answering particular questions. This greatly intrigued him. He hypothesized that there is a developmental progression to intellectual growth. Piaget began to believe that how children think is much more important and more revealing of their mental ability than tabulating what they know (Flavell, 1963). Moreover, understanding how children think also reveals how they interpret their experiences and gradually construct their understanding of the world (Berger, 1994).

In the 1950's Piaget developed his stages of cognitive development. His work revolutionized our understanding of the way that individuals make sense of the world. To develop his theory, Piaget utilized children of all ages. He used the clinical method to gather data. That is, he posed a problem for children and observed and recorded their solutions. In his stages, Piaget asserted that our process of thinking changes, as we get older, as we strive to make sense of the world.

Knowledge and perception are key words in Piagetian theory. With regards to knowledge, it is a process involving individuals acting upon or with the environment – both mentally and physically. Perception is a child's view of the world, which can be a tinted, biased lens. The lens is affected by past experiences and a child's current stage of development (Berger, 1994).

PIAGET'S STAGES OF COGNITIVE DEVELOPMENT

STAGE ONE: *Sensorimotor* (Birth – 2 years). Infants use their senses and motor abilities to make sense of the world. There are two landmark concepts during this stage. 1. *Object Permanence:* The infant learns that objects still exist even when they are not in sight. 2. *Differed Imitation:* The infant observes an event (i.e., someone opening a door by turning the knob) and they remember.

STAGE TWO: *Preoperational* (2-6 years). The child utilizes symbolic thinking to make sense of the world, including language. In the early portions of the stage the child can be *egocentric* (seeing only their own point of view) in nature. The key to this stage is that the child's imagination flourishes. He/she is able to engage in self-expression via language. In addition, they become *decentered* (open to multiple points of view).

STAGE THREE: *Concrete Operations* (7-11 years). During this stage the child is capable of developing certain logic. Tangible (concrete) reasoning is also apparent. A key concept during stage three is *conservation:* if a form changes its contents do not. An example of this concept, made "famous" by Piaget would be as follows:

Two cups of equal size are filled with the same volume of water. Assume that a child from each of the last two stages measures the cups to ensure they are holding the same amount of water. The cups are then poured into two different glasses: one tall and thin, the other short and wide. Obviously, the water goes towards the top of the taller thinner glass, while it does not make it halfway up the shorter, wider glass. If asked which glass has the most water, a child in stage two (preoperational stage) should point to the tall, thinner glass. A child in stage three (concrete operations) will know that the glasses hold the same amount of water.

STAGE FOUR: *Formal Operations* (11 years – adulthood). This is a period of abstract reasoning, based on verbal and logical statements. Social and moral issues, as well as ethics and politics, become more motivating and involving to the adolescent. During this stage the individual can construct organizational convictions, taking a more broad (more hypothetical) approach to experience.

Even though ages are attached to the aforementioned stages, they should not be considered anything more than approximations. Piaget, himself, noted this:

They are not stages which can be given a chronological date. On the contrary, the ages can vary from one society to another......But there is a constant order of succession, that is, in order to reach a certain stage, previous steps must be taken (Piaget, 1973, p. 10-11).

Paiget, like Erikson, believed that in order to advance to the next stage, one must complete the current stage. In our work within the milieu, we have come to realize that a child's chronological age does not always match their mental age. This is why Piaget's stages are a useful tool. They can help us identify a child's cognitive abilities, not making an assessment based on chronology, but rather their mental ability. Much of the practical use of Piaget's findings for educators and parents (and residential workers) lies in his identification of approximate age levels at which the maturation needed for developing particular schemes or intellectual operations occur (Thomas, 1992). If the necessary maturation has not transpired, it is pointless to try to teach the child a particular skill.

KOHLBERG AND MORAL DEVELOPMENT

Influenced by the work of Piaget, Lawrence Kohlberg also was interested in the study of cognitive development. However, and in addition, Kohlberg studied the development of moral reasoning in individuals. He did this by presenting children and adolescents (as well as adults) with a series of hypothetical stories that pose ethical problems. The most famous of these imaginary examples that Kohlberg (1963) utilized is the story of Heinz:

A woman was near death from cancer. One drug might save her, a form of radium, that a druggist in the same town had recently discovered. The druggist was charging $2,000 for the drug, ten times what it had cost him to make. The sick woman's husband, Heinz, went to everyone he knew to borrow the money, but he could only come up with half of the amount. He told the druggist that his wife was dying and asked him to sell it cheaper or let him pay later. But the druggist said, "no." The husband became desperate and broke into the man's store to steal the drug for his wife. Should the husband have done that? Why?

When Kohlberg would examine responses to dilemmas such as the aforementioned, he found that there were three levels to moral reasoning: pre-conventional, conventional and post-conventional (Berger, 1994). Each of these levels had two stages. They are as follows:

I. PRE-CONVENTIONAL: The emphasis during this level is on avoiding punishments and getting rewards.

Stage One: "Might makes right." The most important value during this stage is obedience to authority so that punishment is avoided.

Stage Two: "Look out for number one." Each individual tries to take care of his or her own needs. The lesson during this stage is that if you are nice to other people they will be nice to you (i.e.: "you scratch my back and I'll scratch yours).

II. CONVENTIONAL: The emphasis during this level is on social rules.

Stage Three: "What a good Boy." "What a nice girl." Individuals learn that good behavior is behavior that pleases other people. It wins their praise. At this stage, approval is more important than rewards.

Stage Four: "Law and order." The right behavior means being a compliant citizen, following the laws set down by those in authority.

III. POST-CONVENTIONAL: The emphasis during this level is on moral principles.

Stage Five: "Social contract." The rules of society are created to benefit all. They are established by mutual agreement. If the rules become unhelpful, or if a party does not abide by the agreement, the contract is no longer binding.

Stage Six: "Universal ethical principles." Commonly held principles determine right and wrong. These values (i.e., "do unto others as you would have others do unto you") are established through individual reflection, and may contradict the egocentric or legal principles of earlier reasoning.

APPLYING MORAL DEVELOPMENT TO CHILDREN IN RESIDENTIAL PLACEMENT

It could be stated that children who enter residential placement, especially those who are younger, are in the lower stages of Kohlberg's moral development model. This is especially true if we look at the pre-conventional level (stage one) in which youth learn that "might makes right." How many children enter placement with a fear of adult power and control? They may have learned to *be obedient or else*. However, *being obedient* as they learned the phrase in an abusive home, is vastly different than what is acceptable in our society. Residential staff members must show these children that power and control (abuse) should never be mandates for adhering to the rules (of the milieu, society, etc.). Rather, the penalty for not following rules will result in social sanctions (isolation, alienation, etc.). Children should be taught to follow the rules because the rules are fair to all – not because children will be beaten if they don't.

In stage two of the pre-conventional level, we are back to having needs met. Often, especially if they came from an abusive environment, *looking out for number one* means keeping safe. It is hard to have other needs met if a child is constantly trying to ensure his/her safety. Therefore (as asserted throughout chapter three) residential staff can help these children to have their needs met. In addition, it is also imperative for staff members to show children that giving kindness to others will be reciprocated. Children should be taught that helping others, and being kind to them is not just an exercise in futility.

DIFFERENT LEARNING STYLES IN YOUTH

Just as there are different stage development theories (psychosocial, cognitive, moral, etc.) we can apply to childhood development, we should not ignore the fact that children learn differently, too. Some youth respond to verbal instruction, some need visual aids, and some even have to involve their bodies in learning (Wisconsin Education Association, 1996). In order for us to be successful in our work with youth, we sometimes need to step back and look at what learning style is best for the individual child. The Wisconsin Education Association (1996) states that a learning style is usually evident in children by the age of seven, and understating a child's learning style can help residential staff, clinicians, and teachers to:

a. Help children think and learn to the best of their abilities.
b. Understand behaviors that might stand in the way of learning.

A proactive and creative way to review some of the learning styles of children is described by Dawna Markova, Ph.D. through the Wisconsin Education Association (1996) as the **Six Learning Styles**:

1. *Showers and Tellers:* Natural persuaders who learn best through reading and light up when telling stories.
2. *Seers/Feelers:* Empathetic children who learn best by doing what they are shown and asking endless questions.

3. *Leaders of the Pack:* Natural powerhouses who learn by teaching others. Though they have extensive speaking vocabularies, they tend to have difficulty learning to read and write.
4. *Verbal Gymnasts:* Effective and articulate communicators whose words pour out in logical order. They love facts and history and ideas of all kinds, and have to talk to understand.
5. *Wandering Wanderers:* Quiet Einsteins who learn best in solitude. Can learn physical tasks easily without verbal instruction. Can become overwhelmed by listening.
6. *Movers and groovers:* Athletes who need to be allowed to use their bodies in order to learn – often labeled hyperactive. Reading and writing may be very difficult.

There is no doubt that many of these learning styles apply to children in residential placement. In my prior work in residential programs, I worked with youth I could identify as *verbal gymnasts, quiet Einsteins,* and *movers and groovers.* This segment was designed to point out that learning styles not only apply to youth in care, but that staff members accept that all children learn differently. There is not one standard mold. Just as residential workers need to understand healthy childhood development theories, they must understand which learning styles work best for the individual child.

Wrapping It All Up

The other day I was reviewing some stories I had written when I was in high school. I chuckled aloud because they were full of common adolescent themes, such as:
- My parents were not understanding of me.
- I was unattractive.
- My rebellion against my parents, my boss at work, etc., was justified.
- The future was not clear.

We know these themes are common in adolescence. In residential programs we must never forget that. My parents didn't overly punish me when I was struggling to find my place in this world. While there were times when I needed to be grounded on a Friday night, they did not *throw the book at me* and were sympathetic to my growing pains.

In residential placement it is too easy to forget the growing pains of adolescence, especially when workers do not receive proper support from their agency. When I was disrespectful to my parents as a teenager, I was not placed on unending restriction. Nor was I challenged to a verbally escalating debate until it ended up in a restraint. Lastly, I was not shunned by the caretakers in my life. Adolescence is a difficult developmental stage for the youth and the adults in their life. In the milieu it is additionally difficult because a staff's improper responses can make it more painful than it has to be.

Nobody can deny that teenage angst is a difficult time for both youth and adults. That is why knowledge of this stage is important. But the other stages are just as important. Sometimes all we have to do is remember back to our own childhood. We innately know what is "normal" and what isn't. Sometimes reading what has been written about a particular stage is also helpful. It helps to keep us focused on our jobs.

This has been a very elementary introduction into stage development (and learning styles). Erikson, Piaget and Kohlberg were highlighted because their theories have "stood the test of time." More importantly, in this brief presentation, all of these individuals believed that the environment in which the individual lives greatly influences their development. This is important in our work: we have to understand that the child's environment within the milieu plays a major role in that youngster's development. Residential workers can assist in promoting healthy development – or they can inhibit the process. Residential workers can help a child "catch up" in maladaptive developmental growth – or they can stunt it.

CHAPTER FIVE
Issues of Grief, Loss and Trauma

"Grief shared is grief diminished."
Rabbi Grollman

Children in residential placement have been removed from their families of origin. In some instances, their families abandoned them. Regardless, they are sometimes placed in residential care, away from their families, and they have no idea of when or if they will ever return home. No matter how short the length of stay in a residential placement may be, these youth are separated from those they were most connected to. It is logical that youngsters in this predicament would feel a sense of loss. As stated in earlier chapters, workers must remember that behaviors are signals of inner turmoil and pain.

Trauma is another antecedent to children's residential placement. Children carry the physical and emotional scars of traumatic episodes. Combined with the issues of grief and loss, a residential worker's job just gets tougher. It is the staff members that work in the residential unit that will have a great impact in helping children deal with their issues of grief, loss, and trauma.

GRIEF AND LOSS FOR CHILDREN IN CARE

Children in care know they're different. If they go to public schools this disparity is even more intensified. In a story of second-grade children who were told that one of their classmates was adopted, the most common response was "I'm sorry." (Paddock, 2002). Imagine the child who isn't adopted. Imagine what it must feel like to lose your parents and then have to face the realization that not only were you abandoned, but also that nobody else seems to wants you. Such are the feelings of loss that many children in care face. They have lost their birth parents and will have to confront the reality that painful, sad things can happen to them (Paddock, 2002).

When one investigates issues of loss for youth placed in protective care they ascertain that one of the first feelings a child will express is that it was his/her fault. Many feel that they were the reason they lost their parents. There is this incredible void in their lives and the children believe they are responsible for the chasm. That is why residential staff members must make the milieu a place to which the child feels connected. We need to embrace our children, nurture their hopes and dreams, show them opportunity, and guide them through struggle and challenges (Allen, 2002).

Caring compassionate adults are cornerstones in helping youth deal with grief. Its stages are not linear. There will be good days and not so good days. Shock, denial, anger, regression, guilt, bargaining and finally acceptance are the myriad of emotions that are part of the healing process called grief (Zotovich, 2000). Three of the more common signs that residential staff should expect to witness in grieving children are:

- Anger
- Withdrawal
- Anxiety

An appropriate way for staff to help children with these issues is to assure them that what they are feeling is okay. Dee Paddock (2002), a counselor from Colorado, believes:

The approach of caring adults should be to validate the child's experience by talking about it – first, name the feeling that's going on – anger, depression, anxiety – then check it out with the child. You can help them find ways to cope. Let them know they are not foolish or uncaring if they feel sad or angry or fearful. No one can make these children's losses smaller by suppressing them. Caring adults can, however, help them to make the rest of their lives bigger (p.2).

WAYS TO HELP CHILDREN COPE

The following section is complete with tips for helping children cope with feelings of grief and loss. They are listed here to appeal to a wide audience. The material can be utilized to help a child new to residential placement, as well as a child who has experienced (another) significant loss. As with other portions of this book, consult with your agency's clinical team if there are any questions regarding this information. The following tips come from the *National Association of School Psychologists* (NASP) (2001).

- ***Allow children to be the teachers of their grief experiences.*** Give children the opportunity to tell their story and be a good listener.

- ***Grieving is a process, not an event.*** Programs need to allow adequate time for a child to grieve in the manner that works best for that child. Pressing children to resume "normal" activities without the chance to deal with their emotional pain may prompt additional problems or negative reactions.

- ***Don't lie or tell half-truths to children about the tragic event.*** Children are often bright and sensitive. They will see through false information and wonder why you do not trust them with the truth. Lies do not help the child through the healing process or help develop effective coping strategies for life's future tragedies and losses.

- ***Don't assume that children always grieve in an orderly or predictable way.*** We all grieve in different ways and there is no one "correct" way for people to move through the grieving process. (As highlighted in the chapter on development, a child's chronological age does not mean that he/she will grieve in the exact way as another youth of the same age.)

- ***Let children know that you really want to understand what they are feeling or what they need.*** Sometimes children are upset but they cannot tell you what will be helpful. Giving them time and encouragement to share their feelings with you may enable them to sort out their feelings.

- ***Children will need long lasting support.*** The more losses the child or adolescent suffered, the more difficult it will be to recover.

- ***Keep in mind that grief is hard work.*** This is true regardless of age.

Being a Good Listener

The first tip listed in this section involves being a good listener. We are used to hearing that this attribute is beneficial for workers in our field. However, being a good (effective) listener is not as easy as one would think. It is not simply sitting down and allowing the child to pour their heart out. We all are aware of ways *not to* practice good listening skills. We know the scene of a child rushing into to tell his dad about something exciting that happened at the park. The only problem is that dad is watching the news. Even when he turns to face his son, it is evident that he is not really listening.

Many of us say that we are good listeners. But, do we really know the techniques involved and how to apply them? According to the Canadian Association of Student Activity Advisors (CASAA) (1999), people need to practice and acquire skills to be a good listener. Some guidelines, as adapted from the work of CASAA (1999), include:

- *Act like a good listener.* In our modern culture, we have learned to turn away a good deal of information that is propelled towards us. It therefore becomes important to us to change our physical bodies from that of a deflector to a receiver. Since our face contains most of the receptive equipment of our bodies, it is natural that the first step in acting like a good listener is to turn our faces towards the channel of information.

- *Look at the other person talking to you.* This will allow your eyes to pick up all the non-verbal signs people send out when they are speaking. By looking at the speaker, your eyes will complete the eye contact the speaker is trying to make. A speaker will work harder at sending out information if they see they have a receptive audience.

- *React by sending out non-verbal signs.* Move your face and give the range of emotions that indicate whether or not you are following what the speaker is saying. Look interested and avoid conversation halting gestures, like staring into space, yawning, etc. These actions tell the speaker, "I'm not really interested."

- **Use receptive language**. Avoid the temptation to burst into the conversation. Instead use words like "I see," "Oh, really," etc. that follow and encourage your speaker's train of thought. This will force you to react to the ideas presented instead of the person. You can then move to asking questions as opposed to stating your opinion. It is a true listening skill to use your mouth as a moving receptor of information rather than a broadcaster.

- **Concentrate on what the speaker is saying**. You cannot fully hear another's point of view when you are arguing mentally or judging what the person is saying before he/she finishes. An open mind is one that receives and listens to information.

There are other things to remember regarding the art of good listening. The first thing is that you may feel drained after the speaker has finished. Effective listening is an active rather than passive activity (CASSA, 1999). The other tip is that you may find yourself "wandering" away while you are listening to the speaker. If this is happening, you might want to alter your body position. Your body position tells whether you are being a good listener – or whether you are just simply deflecting information. You just can't fake your way through being an effective listener. People know if you are interested or not.

This section on listening skills does not apply solely to listening to grieving children. It can be utilized for life in general. Its inclusion in this text is to help you think about whether you are a good listener or not, and whether you want to be. Being able to assist people in need is based upon the premise that the helper is truly concerned about the well being of others. In our jobs, listening to what children are saying is an important skill. We cannot tell a child that we know what he/she is feeling. We have to let the youngster express his/her feelings. And, we have to be willing to listen.

Creativity Can be Used to Express Feelings

Being creative can also help youngsters deal with the grieving process. One way to help children express their internal pain is through artwork. If a child cannot verbalize feelings, he/she may be able to draw them. (Even those who can express their feelings through words sometimes find it easier to draw pictures.) When the drawing or other piece of artwork is completed, the staff member may then have the opportunity to explore the child's feelings by talking about the art. The youth may not want to talk. That is okay. Eventually they will.

In the interim, the staff member can bring the artwork to the child's clinician. If the child does want to talk about his or her drawing at the residence, the staff member should not shut him/her out. Staff can make some general comments such as, "I hear what you're saying" or "You know this picture shows the feelings you're telling me about. You did a great job." The staff member can then say, "You know, I really appreciate your telling me about these feelings. And, I also think Susan (the child's clinician) would like to see the picture and hear you explain it."

An additional way for children to express grief is to write about it. For some children keeping a journal is a wonderful way to facilitate the grieving process (Zotovich, 2000). While this creative approach may also require clinical intervention, there is nothing prohibiting residential workers from encouraging children to write down what they are feeling. This will encourage the child to state what is going on and (hopefully) give them a way to process feelings without acting out with frustration and anger in the milieu. In addition, it could alleviate the potential of the child becoming withdrawn at the residence.

Children need to have an outlet to express their feelings. Writing in a journal – or drawing pictures – gives them such an outlet. And, like the drawing, the journal can then be brought to the child's clinician for processing. (If the child wants the residential staff to read it, the same verbal cues can be used as with the artwork. It all depends on how comfortable the staff member feels, and what the agency team has decided in regards to staff-child "therapy.") It should be noted here that *a child's journal is private* – and the staff do not automatically have a right to read it. It is the child's choice as to whether staff can read the journal.

Being creative, a good listener, and knowing the signs of a child grieving a loss can make a residential worker an important helper. In an earlier chapter, the notion of one caring adult being vital in the life of a child was related. In no instance is this truer than in assisting a child dealing with grief and loss. The single most important factor that helps grieving youth to become emotionally adjusted and competent adults is the active involvement of at least one adult who cares

(Edelman, 1998). As caring adults, we must be listening to and watching for, at all times, what children say and don't say. Residential workers must be ready to help when children are calling them. Having a good listener hear their feelings is the first thing that children need to begin their expression (and hopefully, alleviation) of grief.

SYMPTOMS OF TRAUMA

There are many forms of trauma and many ways in which it is experienced. Modern life does not lack for trauma producing events (Matsakis, 1998). There are numerous ways in which it is experienced. Trauma survivors are those individuals who, at one or at many points in their lives, were rendered helpless and trapped in situations of great danger (Matsakis, 1998). It is not unusual for individuals to develop a wide range of adaptive responses to cope with their trauma (Brohl, 1996). Some examples of incidents causing trauma include:

- Loss of a family member of other important person
- Physical, sexual and/or emotional abuse
- Natural disasters
- Parental separation and/or divorce
- Accidental injuries (burns, severe cuts, etc.)
- Witnessing:
  a. Domestic violence
  b. Murder, rape or suicidal behavior
  c. Automobile accidents

This list could continue with other horrors of our modern day, including terrorist attacks. The world is a changed and frightening place for children today (Brohl, 1996). It is also clear that the youth we care for have experienced one or more examples cited on the aforementioned list. All children and adolescents in residential placement have experienced some form of loss and/or trauma (Pomfret, In Press, 2002). This is not unexpected in our field.

The chart below reflects trauma statistics due to child abuse and neglect in my home state of Rhode Island in 2000. The chart is straightforward and easy to follow. An encapsulated review will show that a total of 13,580 reports/calls were made to the *Department of Children, Youth and Families* in Rhode Island, the nation's smallest state. The Department investigated over half of these calls and found credible evidence in excess of 20% of the cases. 91% of the abuse and neglect cases involved victim's parents, relatives or other household members. Sadly, three (3) children died in Rhode Island as a direct result of abuse in 2000. (National statistics for 1999 appear in chapter six.)

CHILD ABUSE AND NEGLECT IN RHODE ISLAND
(FOR CALENDAR YEAR 2000)

- There were 13,580 total number unduplicated child maltreatment reports/calls to the RI Department of Children, Youth and Families (DCYF) Hotline.

- DCYF completed 7,635 investigations as a result of those reports/calls.

- DCYF found credible evidence in a total of 2,731 cases (indicated) involving 3,060 children.

- Of the Calendar Year 2000 cases (3,060), 1,102 were under the age of 5 years and of these 214 were infants under the age of 1 year.

- 69% of indicated cases were by neglect, 19% were by physical abuse, 7% sexual abuse, 2% medical neglect, 1% emotional abuse, and 3% other.

- 37% of the child neglect victims were because of a lack of adult supervision.

- 91% of the abuse was perpetrated by the victim's parents, relatives or other household members.

- Between 1990 and 2000, 43 children died as a direct result of abuse by a parent or caretaker – 3 in 2000.

Information Source: *Prevent Child Abuse Rhode Island*

Post-Traumatic Stress Disorder

With all that is happening in our society, it is no wonder that the children and adolescents we work with are in such traumatic states. Many of them suffer from Post-Traumatic Stress Disorder (PTSD), an anxiety disorder that arises after a child has experienced an episode of trauma. The symptoms commonly occur one to three months after the incident. The major standard for experiencing PTSD is that the person has experienced an event that is outside the range of usual human existence that would be markedly distressing to almost anyone (Pomfret, In Press, 2002). The event is continually experienced by the child, and there is a noted "avoidance" associated with the incident. Symptoms of increased arousal persist that were not present before the trauma.

PTSD was introduced in 1980 in the *Diagnostic and Statistical Manual of Mental Disorders* (DSM-III) of the American Psychiatric Association. However, consistent patterns of psychological distress following such sudden traumatic experiences, such as natural disasters or combat horror had been described in both professional and popular literature for many years prior to the formal inclusion of PTSD in the DSM-III (Foy, 1992). Many of these traumatic experience involved veterans of World Wars, whereby we became acquainted with the terms "shell shock" and "combat fatigue."

The disorder arose further into the national spotlight during the 1980's. This was when stories of many Viet Nam veterans experiencing flashbacks, night terrors and other incidents began to surface. Given the traumatic events related by veterans of this war, it is no wonder that many of them experience the disorder. It is also easy to understand why so many Viet Nam veterans needed clinical treatment to help them alleviate some of their trauma.

Trauma that remains untreated can have the most detrimental impact on an individual. An example of how children can experience trauma is evidenced in the words of Dr. John Sieta, et al. (1996). Dr. Seita grew up in residential care after being removed from his family at a young age:

As a five-year-old, I watched my father beat my mother. I witnessed him bang her head repeatedly against the wall. I saw blood and heard her scream out that she was "seeing stars" and that he "may as well go ahead and kill her." Then suddenly he stopped beating her and loaded us into an old blue Pontiac and took her, in a dazed and bloodied condition, to the hospital emergency room for medical care. I was confused and terrified (p. 4).

Those of us who have worked in this field for any length of time have gotten used to these stories. In some instances workers have become "sensitized" to them. Nothing shocks us anymore. However, PTSD is very treatable. It is one symptom that our field has had much practice with. As this portion of the chapter serves as a brief overview of Post-Traumatic Stress Disorder, we will now focus on:

a. Symptoms of PTSD
b. Managing PTSD Symptoms Within the Milieu

SYMPTOMS OF PTSD

The symptoms of this disorder are numerous. Some of the intrusive symptoms (Pomfret, In Press, 2002) include:
- Nightmares of the event or other traumatic dream
- Invasive memories and images
- Sounds and smells embedded in the child's brain

It is also common for children to recreate the behavior symptomatic of the trauma. That is, children can be *melodramatic in response to environmental stimuli.* (This can sometimes be mistaken for ADHD.) They can also *become very upset when they experience reminders of the trauma.*

Getting back to sound, one might wonder how this can become symptomatic. An example of how sound, in this case music, can impact an individual, even years after the trauma was experienced, is related in a book by Robert McNamara (1999) entitled, *Beating the Odds*. Dr. McNamara is another individual who grew up in the child welfare system. Even now, some twenty years after he experienced trauma, Dr. McNamara states that music from the 1970's era can depress him. He remembers:

I used music as a way to escape much of what was happening to me at the time. I remember sitting on my bed for hours listening to the songs of the group Chicago on an old eight-track player I salvaged from the garbage. I would try to imagine I was somewhere else while listening to the music of Donna Summer, Billy Joel, Aerosmith,

Manfred Mann, the Beach Boys, the Doobie Brothers, or James Taylor. For those moments I was able to escape the emotional stress of my living situation. To hear those songs today, however, brings back many of those painful memories (p. 155-156).

When working with children and adolescents who are diagnosed with PTSD there are two other symptoms that should be mentioned briefly. The first symptom is *distrust*. Distrustful youth need to see to believe. They have been "burned" before. Vacations have been cancelled due to a family accident. A child's dad has returned to visit his daughter, promising her that things will be different – and then he molests her. The list could go on. Children with PTSD can become overly cautious, challenging staff with words like, "I'll believe it when I see it."

Another PTSD symptom to be covered in this chapter is that of youth exhibiting *high-risk behavior*. This conduct can be utilized to mask other symptoms, such as depression, fear, or anxiety. Adolescents seem to be the age group that exhibits this behavior. They can become sexually promiscuous, ignoring all warnings. They may also rebuke authority and challenge staff members. The most difficult thing in dealing with this behavior is that adolescents will in fact take risks and may do great harm to themselves or others in the process.

I remember a peer recalling to me the story of a teenager suffering from PTSD. The child unexpectedly (and unbeknownst to staff) climbed out of his bedroom window and onto the roof of the facility. He was wearing a (makeshift) blue cape, red shorts with blue sweatpants underneath, and high top sneakers. Looking down at the cars passing on the street below, he yelled out, "I am Super Mack." Upon hearing this proclamation a staff member went outside and began to try to reason with the adolescent. Two staff members stayed inside with the other children, trying to keep them occupied with a movie and popcorn. After a half an hour the staff member was able to get the youth to come down from the roof. (Though this episode ended uneventfully, youth exhibiting high-risk behavior might think nothing of jumping into a busy street and making a game out of dodging moving vehicles.)

This last example of PTSD-related behavior may be the most distressing of all for the staff member. The actions of a youth (such as related above) can lead one to wonder if the youth is contemplating suicide. It is not something that can be taken lightly given the symptomology of the youth that we work with. It is even more disconcerting for staff members who are working with adolescents that have a history of depression and self-injurious behavior(s). The signs listed below are things to look for when suspecting a child as suicidal.

SUICIDE WARNING SIGNS
(Kathryn Brohl, 1996)

- The child uncharacteristically gives away prized possessions.
- The child expresses the following emotions excessively and/or for more than a few days: worry, hopelessness, irritability, sorrow, and euphoria.
- The child describes a suicide plan.
- The child makes statements such as "No one really cares about me," "They'll be better off without me," or "Life isn't worth living."
- The child describes his or her funeral.
- The child is psychologically vulnerable due to loss through death, divorce, romantic relationship, friends, moving, or disappointment.
- The child uncharacteristically isolates himself/herself from other people.
- The child's appearance declines.
- The child exhibits uncharacteristic high-risk behavior.
- The child has attempted suicide before.
- The child has been abusing drugs and/or alcohol.

This list serves only as a guide for staff working with PTSD youth in the milieu. As it is just a listing of potential signs of suicidal behavior, workers should consult with their clinical team if they have concerns regarding a youth's behavior. It is better to make a report that is unsubstantiated than not one at all. There is no such thing as a foolish report. As stated throughout this text, nobody knows the child in residential placement better than the direct care staff.

Managing PTSD Symptoms Within the Milieu

Just as adults need to be aware of PTSD symptoms when working with traumatized children, they must also be versed in the day-to-day management of these youth. According to Pomfret (In Press, 2002), some factors to consider include:
- The effects of trauma will not just simply dissipate when the environment changes.
- Children can suppress feelings for short time frames but feelings and behavior will likely recur.
- Children who are unable to experience emotions will act out on them nonetheless.
- During bedtime or other quiet times, children may demonstrate more acting out behavior. Bedtime can be a source of anxiety for children in residential placement. Many youth in residential placement have experienced abuse during the evening – or in their bedroom. Staff will be challenged in making sure these children feel safe at bedtime. (Some suggestions to help with an anxious child at bedtime might include a *chart program*, whereby a child earns a check for each night of the week he or she goes to bed without any problems. At the end of the week, if enough checks were earned, the child would receive later bedtime on the weekend.)

Most importantly, it is essential to be aware of safety between children, especially in relationship to violent or sexually acting out behavior with their peers. As discussed in earlier chapters, children in our care will act out behaviorally. While these behaviors offer the opportunity to help children, staff members must be on alert for children engaging in physical confrontations and sexual relations. Sexual relations between children and youth in care is not unheard of by any means. In fact, it is a common issue for abused and traumatized children. Their reactive behavior can draw clients towards each other. They may have lived in a home whereby sexual relations between child-child or child-adult were considered *normal*. Staff in the residential milieu must always be on the lookout for such behavior. A high level of supervision of the children can never be underscored.

SECONDARY TRAUMA – COMPASSION FATIGUE

There is a cost that comes for caring for children who have suffered severe trauma. Those who work with children in residential placement, listening to stories of pain and fear, may themselves feel similar fear and pain. Professionals who work with children who have suffered trauma must contend not only with the normal stresses of their work but also with the emotional feelings for the suffering. This is commonly referred to as compassion fatigue. (We may also know this condition by various other names, such as *secondary* or *vicarious trauma*.) In the last few years there has been much professional literature devoted to the emerging condition of compassion fatigue in the helping profession.

Compassion fatigue is not burnout. Burnout is associated with stress and annoyances involved at work. It is predictable and can often be cured with a vacation. Compassion fatigue is a condition of anxiety and concern with the individual or collective trauma of clients visible in one or more ways, including re-experiencing the traumatic event, evading reminders of the event, and constant stimulation. With compassion fatigue staff absorbs the trauma through the eyes and ears of the children in care.

There are three risk factors that workers in the helping profession must be aware of that can lead to a form of secondary trauma (compassion fatigue):

1. Exposure to stories (or images) of children severely traumatized.
2. An individual's empathetic sensitivities to a child's suffering.
3. Any unresolved emotional issues that relate to the suffering seen.

There is little that a professional who works with children in residential placement can do about the first two risk factors. However, workers can reduce the risk for compassion fatigue if they know their own personal vulnerabilities and unresolved issues. When workers feel that the issues a particular child is relating has the potential to impart secondary trauma on them (the adult), that staff member should ask a peer for assistance. It is also important for this staff member to seek professional help to deal with unresolved issues. (The Appendix includes a list of websites for professionals in our field and includes a site on secondary traumatization.)

Another way that workers can receive help in combating compassion fatigue is through *debriefing groups* with the agency team. This is a chance for the clinical team to help those who are "on the front lines" with children in the residential setting. While these group sessions (they should be voluntary – not mandatory) can help many, sometimes individual sessions are also necessary. Agencies/clinicians should make sure that there are times for staff members to talk about what is going on in the milieu environment and how it is affecting them.

TIPS FOR (STAFF) STRESS REDUCTION

Just as our work can lead to compassion fatigue, our labors can also lead to high levels of stress. After all, the traumatized children that we work with bring many of their problems to our attention. They are looking for us to help them deal with their pains and fears. This can bring a fair amount of stress into our professional lives. There are ways that professionals in our field can deal with this stress. The *Canadian Mental Health Association* (CMHA) (2001) recommends the following tips for staff members dealing with stress:
- Recognize your symptoms of stress (you know your body better than anyone).
- Use relaxation techniques (meditation, deep breathing, massage).
- Exercise (physical activities is one of the best stress remedies available).
- Talk (with friends, counselors, support groups) about what is bothering you.
- Get enough rest and sleep.
- Watch your diet (alcohol, caffeine, sugar, fats and tobacco strain a body's ability to cope with stress).

These suggestions are intended to help the professional deal with the stress that can come with the job. They are suggestions only. The direct care worker, supervisor, or clinician (as individual professionals in the children's residential placement field) are the only ones who can decide when and if (personal) emotions are being caused by job-related stress or secondary trauma as a result of unresolved issues from one's own life. In this instance, talking with a professional counselor might be a good choice.

NEXT STEPS

There is no doubting the advances our field has made in working with children in residential placement. We have seen a growth in literature defining new concepts that have been developed to help us in our work. This chapter has briefly reviewed some of these theoretical concepts, including: Post Traumatic Stress Disorder (PTSD) and Compassion Fatigue. PTSD has been a *mainstream practice* for just under three decades. Compassion Fatigue, itself, is gaining much recognition as a concept. It is rapidly becoming known as an accepted "cost" of working within the human services field.

Likewise, we know that children's residential placement is making many advances in the treatment of traumatized youth. Our field has established a role within our society. We need to keep this forward movement going. The next chapter will build upon this theme, looking at our field as a whole. It will challenge us to look at the opportunities we have to help families in care. As family-centered practice becomes commonplace in our work, this concept will greatly impact residential work. It will help us "complete the job" we started.

CHAPTER SIX
Working with the Families of Children in Care

"What children expect from grownups is not to be "understood" but only to be loved, even though this love may be expressed clumsily or in sternness."
Carl Sucker

Children crave the loving approval of their parents. Those who work in residential placement facilities know this better than anyone. Whether or not their parents showed affection or were abusive or neglectful, children still yearn to be with them. While residential placement facilities play an important role in our society, we have to play an even bigger role in helping families *make it*. Families do not always have to lose their child to the system. When a child is placed in care it does not mean that an agency should work exclusively with the child, at the expense of the family. This is not what the child wants.

Those of us in the field are often put in an uncomfortable situation. We work with youngsters who come from unstable, sometime abusive environments. We help ease the transition, making the child feel safe. We provide these children with the basics and give him/her nurturance. Then we watch (and hope) as the child is reunified with his family. As much as we want families to be reunited, sometimes it can be hard for them. That is why we need to work so diligently with both the child and their family during a youngster's placement. In doing so we may be able to help ensure a successful transition.

Sometimes, however, it seems as if the adults in a child's life are engaged in an endless feud. Residential programs, families, state and county departments (as well as advocates) can sometimes lose focus as to what is actually in the child's best interest. On occasion these adults engage in territorial debates as to what is the best course of action for the youngster. When these happens nobody wins – least of all the child.

DON'T CONDEMN A CHILD'S PARENTS (HELP THEM)

This text has frequently stated that staff members should never condemn a child's family. These youth are in residential placement to receive treatment – and treatment is *always* compromised if professionals, in any manner, demean a child's family. Many residential staff members have witnessed firsthand the old adage that "blood is thicker than water." Children love their parents. They may harbor negative feelings as well, but the love rarely dies. As a result, most children in out-of-home placements will jump at the opportunity to return home to the parents who have abused and/or neglected them, hoping that they are doing better and will love them. Our jobs are to help every child and his/her family establish the best relationship they can. If reunification is possible, that's great. But even if it isn't, a good residential setting will actively help children to accept the *best possible relationship* he/she can have with his/her family, so that he/she is ready to say hello to a new one.

One of the things residential placements can do is to help parents learn how to properly care for their children. When my wife and I were direct care workers, we had a child's mother (and her boyfriend) visit the residence once a week. They would join us for the after school through shower routine. At first Laurie and I were apprehensive. Our two big concerns were:

1. How would it feel disciplining the child in front of his parents?
2. How would the children who didn't have family feel about a peer having his mother join us once a week for five hours?

Our initial concern was alleviated on the first night before dinner. The child's clinician came out to talk with all the adults and encouraged Laurie and I to go about things as usual. The child's mother and her boyfriend would stay in the kitchen to simply listen and observe. His mother even told us, "Do what you normally do. Don't worry about me being offended if you have to punish Clarence." This was a great relief. Eventually, we involved Clarence's mother in decisions when he needed to be consequenced. His mom was great. After a couple of weeks she began processing things with him, such as, "Clarence you know you shouldn't be wrestling with the other kids. We've talked about this before. Now, why don't you go take some time in your room, calm down, and think about things?"

In relation to our concerns about the other children's feelings at seeing Clarence's mother coming to the house, we were just as pleasantly surprised. The other boys loved having the company. Just as when my family visited the residence, the children liked to socialize and see that they did not live in a closed world. They began to look forward to her visits. Her boyfriend knew a lot about cars and auto racing. The other boys in the house would love talking with him about hotrods.

There are definite ways that residential placements can help parents prepare for their children's reintegration into the family. Appelstein (1994) suggests the following:

1. Having families spend time in the milieu (as in the aforementioned example), including letting the parents cook meals, attend holiday parties, etc.

2. Institute parent support groups – even while the youth is still in care.

3. Ask parents for their help. This is especially true when a reunification is forthcoming. What is wrong with calling a parent and saying, "Suzy has just pulled the fire alarm in the home and caused quite a commotion. What do you think a good consequence would be?"

4. Help parents attend visits and meetings (pick them up at their homes if necessary.)

There are other ways that we can assist parents, but they require finding the funds to do so. One way would be to ensure that staff from the residential program (who connected with a youngster) can visit that child every two weeks or for the six months after he or she is discharged (Appelstein, 1994). Another way would be to establish temporary family memberships at a community organization (such as the YMCA). This is already occurring in some states and helps the family establish (and maintain) ties to the community.

Residential placements and parents of children in care are not enemies. The opposite is true. We are partners in the child's treatment. Programs need to help parents learn skills to ensure that a child's return home is a success (Appelstein, 2002). The only barriers that separate parents and staff are the ones adults choose to build. Parents, like all of us, have made mistakes. Residential placement agencies can help ensure that these mistakes are not repeated.

ADOPTION AND SAFE FAMILIES ACT OF 1997

A federal law established to clarify issues as they pertain to children and families is the Adoption and Safe Families Act (ASFA) of 1997. However, for an act that took more than two decades to come to fruition, it is surprising that not all professionals in our field are familiar with ASFA or its purpose. This section of the chapter will attempt to explain the intent of ASFA and some of its major provisions.

In 1980 the Child Welfare and Adoption Act (P.L. 96-272) was passed. It was hoped that by combining preventative services for families with the development of permanency planning for children, youth would not wallow in foster care. But in the late 1980s and early 1990s, the needs of families grew more complex, and services usually available to them were not able to keep up with the demand of needy families (U.S. Department of Health and Human Services, 2000). Policymakers intent on combating the causes of child abuse and neglect through prevention and early intervention services for children and families, passed the Family Preservation and Support Services Program in 1993 (U.S. Department of Health and Human Services, 2000). The program gave additional funding to states to provide services aimed at supporting families.

ASFA builds on these earlier laws and chronicles new state initiatives developed to respond to complex issues faced by children and families (U.S. Department of Health and Human Services, 2000). Another intent of ASFA is that it sets time limits for permanency planning. This often equates to a more expedient termination of parental rights so that children are eligible for adoption. This provision is long overdue. Professionals who have spent their entire careers in the field can attest to seeing children enter residential placement at a young age (5-7). But, by the time parental rights are terminated, the child is now a teenager. Suddenly finding adoptive parents is much more difficult. Now there is a time frame for permanency:

> *ASFA requires that states hold the child's first permanency hearing within 12 months (rather than 18 months). Further, it requires that States initiate or join proceedings to terminate parental rights for parents of children who have been in care for 15 of the last 22 months, except in situations in which the child*

is placed with relatives, there is a compelling reason why termination of parental rights is not in the child's best interests, or when the family has not received the services that were put in the case plan (U.S. Department of Health and Human Services, 2000, p.16).

What many professionals like about this provision is that it helps the parents make more timely decisions about their life and that of their child.

Principles and Key Provisions of the Adoption and Safe Families Act of 1997

(U.S. Department of Health and Human Services, 2000)

- The safety of children is the paramount concern that must guide all child welfare services.

- Foster care is a temporary setting and not a place for children to grow up.

- Permanency planning efforts should begin as soon as the child enters the child welfare system.

- The child welfare system must focus on results and accountability.

<u>Mandatory Provisions</u>

- The focus on safety.

- The 12-month timeline for permanency hearings.

- The requirement for initiating termination of parental rights if a child is in state custody for 15 of the most recent 22 months, unless exceptions apply.

- Health insurance for children with special needs for whom there is an adoption assistance agreement.   *(continued next page)*

> - An expanded focus on family preservation and support programs to include time-limited family reunification and adoption promotion and support services.
>
> - Reports to Congress on selected issues.

ASFA encourages state and county Departments, residential placement agencies, parents, and community based organizations to come together to benefit children and families. The chart below is an encapsulated version of ways in which the field can adhere to the principles of this act.

Critical Questions for Planning to Implement the Provisions of ASFA as they Pertain to Children and Families
(adapted from the resource guide, Rethinking Child Welfare Practice Under the Adoption and Safe Families Act of 1997, U.S. Department of Health and Human Services, 2000)

CHILD FOCUS

1. What strategies are in place to ensure child safety, permanency and well being:
   a. In situations involving family violence, substance abuse, or mental illness?
   b. While ensuring continuity and follow through?
   c. While working to strengthen and support families?

2. What efforts are made to access the overall health and well-being of the child and to access the necessary services to support the child's physical, emotional, and cognitive development while participating in the child welfare system?

3. How is permanency expedited for infants in cases with a poor prognosis for family reunification (e.g., chronic substance abuse, multiple previous removals)?

> **FAMILY-CENTERED SERVICES**
>
> 1. How do an agency's mission, principles, and goals reflect family-centered values?
>
> 2. What strategies are in place to shift the services towards a stronger emphasis on prevention of family crisis, family breakdown and out-of-home placement?
>
> 3. What mechanisms and resources (i.e., financing, organization, manage- ment, staffing, in-service training, family professional partnerships, family advisory boards) are in place to help services become more family-centered?
>
> 4. How are families involved determining how, where, and when services are provided?
>
> 5. What are the strategies to identify, recruit, process, approve, and support qualified foster care and adoptive families?

This section has provided a brief overview of ASFA, its intent, and some key provisions. As states continue to implement the principles of ASFA, the field is left with a guide that will help offer the proper services to children and families. In this regard, ASFA serves as a way to stimulate new thinking in our field.

Family Preservation

For the past two decades, Family Preservation Services (FPS) has made its way into our field at a national level. It constitutes a shift in our thinking, moving towards a practice that is centered on the needs of the family. There are many names for these services (nationally), but the main crux of FPS is based on the premise that children need to be with their families. The other major premise of FPS is that most families, when properly assisted, can care for their children successfully (Child Welfare League of America, 2002). The Child Welfare League of America (CWLA) (2002) notes that the key values of FPS include:

1. Parents and families as a whole are respected.
2. Families have strengths and services should be built on those strengths.
3. Families can take an active role in identifying needs and developing a Service Plan.
4. Services must be flexible, determined by each family's goals.
5. Families are viewed as part of a community.

State or county Departments, in conjunction with private providers (such as residential placement agencies) usually provide FPS. The services are targeted specifically upon the needs of the child and family. They include family counseling, parenting and other skills training, housing assistance, and instruction in family budgeting, stress management, health, nutrition, child development, and behavior management (CWLA, 2002). Another key of FPS is that they may include the opportunity for respite services. This provides parents with a needed break from the child before something negative happens.

According to research conducted by the CWLA (2002), FPS has been attributed to the following outcomes:

Families that have received FPS generally stay together: National evaluations conclude that 80% of families that have received FPS remain together after one year.

FPS has a strong safety record: FPS never advocates leaving a child in an abusive and dangerous situation. The following strategies have lead to FPS' strong safety record:
1. 24-hour referral and response.
2. No waiting period before services begin.
3. Services are provided in the home – caseworkers can monitor danger signals.
4. 24-hour, 7-day-a-week availability of caseworkers to provide support.
5. Caseworkers have the flexibility to respond to and handle emergencies.

Families that have received FPS are doing better: National evaluations have found that FPS has improved parenting skills and affected positive behavioral changes such as improved communication, appropriate discipline, and better care of children.

One of the more encouraging studies on the effectiveness of FPS programs occurred in the state of Oregon. There, the Family Enhancement Program (FEP) was developed by an African American community-based service agency as intensive family preservation services for African American families (Ciliberti, 1998). This innovative program has caseworkers assuming three vital functioning roles: parental, instructional and mentoring. The study compared the outcomes of families served by FEP intervention with families served by the Oregon State Office of Services to Children and Families (SOSCF) (CWLA, 2002). The results of the FEP program in Oregon include:

- The differences between the FEP and SOSCF families at 6 months and 12 months posttest periods were not statistically significant. However, FEP families had fewer placements, fewer days in placement, and fewer founded maltreatment reports (Ciliberti, 1998).

- By the 12-month period, more FEP families were using kinship (relative) care than nonkinship care.

- A decrease in placement days was evident for children in kinship care and nonkinship care when their biological mothers received drug and alcohol services (Ciliberti, 1998).

- Neglecting families showed a relatively high commitment to service utilization, possibly because of the family-based approach (Ciliberti, 1998).

Though this study is highly encouraging, the author noted some of the study's limitations. First of all, the study could not account for maltreating families who had not been identified by state caseworkers (Ciliberti, 1998). The other limitation noted was that generalizations of results to other family preservation programs should be approached carefully because of the unique characteristics of the community in which this particular program was implemented (Ciliberti, 1998).

Aside from these limitations, there are also studies that suggest some family systems do not fair well in FPS. For example, Meezan and McCroskey (1996) studied a project in Los Angeles and found that there was no significant difference in placement rates for children involved with the services (Meezan and McCroskey, 1996). In addition, Schwartz, AuClaire and Harris (1991) conducted research on FPS as an alternative to out-of-home placement. They found that:

> *Thirty-one of the 55 intensive home based service clients had to be removed from their homes. Many were removed several times and for long periods of time. Since a high rate (56.4%) of this group were removed from the home, the study raises the question that perhaps some seriously emotionally disturbed adolescents are not agreeable to home-based interventions and must be placed out-of-home (p. 10).*

REUNIFICATION AND PERMANENCE IS NOT IDEAL IN ALL FAMILIES

Thus far this chapter has reviewed ways to help families of children in placement. This section will balance the chapter by removing any rose colored lenses which lead to blanket statements asserting, "all families should be reunified." Of course, we know this is not true. There are still alarming statistics that reveal (much to our chagrin) children are being victimized within their families at frightening rates.

If one has worked in the field long enough, it is not uncommon to hear of a child who was sent home only to be abused again. More tragically, it is also not out of the question that a worker may have spent time easing a child's nervousness about returning home (even against the youngster's will) only to find that the child has been killed shortly after reunification. These tragedies reaffirm that we have a tough job, and in these tough times we have got to be very diligent in our work.

In *Current Trends in Child Abuse Prevention, Reporting and Fatalities: 1999 Fifty State Survey* published by Prevent Child Abuse America, there are some staggering numbers regarding child maltreatment fatalities. In 1999 an estimated 1,396 children died as a result of child abuse and neglect (Prevent Child Abuse America, 2001). That is nearly four children every day; almost one child every six hours. Children under five years old account for four out of every five fatalities reported, with children under one accounting for two out of every five deaths (Prevent Child Abuse America, 2001). It should be noted that while not all of these deaths occurred in the family unit, a large portion of them did.

Even more troubling is the increase in the number of childhood fatalities during the past decade. Though the Prevent Child Abuse America report is careful to note that some deaths were still under investigation at the time the survey was completed, there has been a steady rise in the number of childhood fatalities due to abuse and neglect. In 1989 there were 685 estimated deaths; in 1995 there were 1,081 estimated deaths; in 1998 there were 1,144 estimated deaths (Prevent Child Abuse America, 2001). In fact, between 1995 and 1999, there was an 11% increase in the number of fatalities due to child abuse and neglect (Prevent Child Abuse America, 2001).

The numbers are horrifying and tend to catch even veteran professionals by surprise. We are accustomed to hearing the media talk about the high cost of residential care. We are accustomed to hearing family advocates talk about how family reunification is better for children and would save states millions of dollars. Both assertions are right. But what we do not often hear is that some children are remaining with or returning to their families, only to be beaten to death or neglected.

The reason for this abuse and neglect of children is due to a multiple factors. The primary presenting problems for abuse and neglect in the aforementioned report are: 1) substance abuse, 2) poverty and economic strains, 3) parental skills and 4) domestic violence (Prevent child Abuse America, 2001). In fact 85% of states liaisons reporting to the survey named substance abuse as one of the top two problems exhibited by families reported for maltreatment; the second most cited problem area involved poverty and economic strains (44%); parental skills and domestic violence were listed as a presenting problem (22% of the time) (Prevent Child Abuse America, 2001).

Data compiled from such reports provides our field with ideas for program designs to help families in crisis. Professionals know that substance abuse treatment is vital. Parenting and anger management programs are also important. While such programs may not directly address socioeconomics, as parents become drug free this can improve the economic condition within the home (i.e., money previously spent on drugs could now be spent on household needs). These approaches (already in place in many FPS programs nationwide) may help us to better assist families.

Parental Deprivation

The last segment contained a review of some of the preventing causes leading to child abuse and neglect. They were substance abuse, poverty and economic strains, parental skills, and domestic violence. Another important factor in our work with children is that many of them come from homes without fathers. Between the soaring divorce rates, "deadbeat dads," and teenage and/or other unexpected pregnancies, too many single mothers are raising their children. This places women at a great financial disadvantage. It also leaves the children without paternal role models.

It is not surprising that many children entering residential placement do not know or have regular contact with, their father. This in itself causes great problems. It is easier for children to go astray without a positive adult male figure in the household. Mothers are much more successful and comfortable setting limits when fathers are present in the household (Lytton, 1979). Mothers who are rearing their children alone experience a great deal of difficulty in disciplining and controlling their children, especially their sons (Hoffman, 1996). However, there is evidence that a high level of paternal involvement, even after a divorce or in the cases when parents never were actually a couple, and a relatively positive mother-father relationship, make the custodial mother's parenting responsibilities more manageable (Wallerstein and Kelly, 1996).

Family work should encompass teaching parents that their relationship, regardless of its status (divorce, separation, irreconcilable), needs to be presented in a positive light to their children. When it comes to family therapy, fathers should be encouraged to participate in the assessment and treatment of the child's problem (Biller and Solomon, 1986). The father's desire to participate should not simply be discarded. This is true even in cases of divorce and separation. If a child has been paternally deprived, a family difficulty (involvement in the child welfare system) may provide the opportunity for getting the father better integrated into the family (Biller and Meredith, 1974). A father's inclusion in treatment is a key factor in much of the success of family therapy (Grebstein, 1986).

ADVOCATING FOR CHILDREN AND FAMILIES: NEW THINKING

Trying to keep families together is worth our best effort. Children long to be loved and accepted by their parents. They have that right. Parents have the right to change negative patterns and atone for their mistakes. Child welfare agencies (such as residential placement facilities) believe that families are not beyond hope, and many families are open to assistance. This is common sense and goes without saying. The more proactive our field can attempt to be, the better.

Putting children and families first (subscribing to family centered practice in our work) is simply a tack away from "older" traditional thinking. It is a conceptual approach – a shift in the way we think about what is helpful for children and families in the child welfare system (National Child Welfare Resource Center for Family-Centered Practice, 2000). In some respects it is finding a common ground between the old guard (families that abuse children are beyond help/respect) and immovable family advocates who believe (the system is responsible for their woes). Putting children and parents first involves helping those who want to make their family better, stronger, and more cohesive. It is our chance to help these individuals one case at a time.

There will be times when families will not be open to assistance, but it still has to be made available to them. Agencies and state/county departments have to extend support. With the implementation of ASFA, there are federally mandated guidelines in place to protect the child and the family unit. So, we can lay down our arms. We can stop the bickering and we can stop pointing fingers. Instead, we can try to help those who want our support and services. Residential placement programs can play a role in the process of helping families becoming healthy again. We can attempt to become a proactive agent of change.

This should be our legacy.

CHAPTER SEVEN
Establishing Diversity in the Milieu

"Behold the turtle. He makes progress only when he sticks his neck out."
James B. Conant

For some time now the field of child welfare has been identifying the need for our profession to grasp issues of ethnicity and diversity. We have attended trainings and entire conferences that focus on the topic. Some agencies have put diversity programs into practice. Many have attempted but are struggling to do so. Other agencies may have simply ignored the premise of diversity, feeling it is unobtainable. However, programmatic diversity is not an agency choice — it must be an agency goal. As the face of America changes, we too, must change the way we look inside and outside of the milieu.

The majority of this chapter will be devoted to ethnic and cultural diversity within the milieu. Our society is changing in leaps and bounds. This forces the human services field to deal with all forms of ethnicity and cultural diversity in order to best serve those we care for. In this light, the first section of the chapter will be devoted to *cultural competence*. Diversity is more than the color of an individual's skin. Rather, it characterizes us as individuals. We must remember this broader definition.

CULTURAL COMPETENCE IN OUR WORK

Cultural diversity is a core part of the economic engine that drives this country, and its impact at this time has significant implications for health care delivery and policymaking throughout the United States (Resources for Cross Cultural Health Care, 1999). We would like to think that we could meet the needs of all those being serviced within our agencies. While our assumptions in our ability to create such an environment may be noble, there are instances wherein this practice does not occur. It happens when there is an ambiguous understanding of what is to be achieved, and how it will be achieved. Therefore, a working definition is needed. Briefly stated, culturally competent services are systems, agencies, and practitioners that have the capacity, skills and knowledge to respond to the unique needs and populations whose cultures are different than that which might be called dominant or mainstream America (Family Resource Coalition, 1996).

Many providers feel they don't have a clear guidance on how to prepare for or respond to situations of cultural diversity. This is not a new problem. It is one that has existed for some time. This has given our field a chance to grasp the issues in order to help our brethren. The Child Welfare League of America (CWLA) established a *Division of Cultural Competence*. It was created to promote new ways of thinking to gain an understanding of cultural competence and its significance to the populations we serve.

The CWLA (2001) defines **cultural competence** as:
the ability of individuals and systems to respond respectfully and effectively to people of all cultures, classes, races, ethnic backgrounds, sexual orientations, and faiths or religions in a manner that recognizes, affirms, and values the worth of individuals, families, tribes, communities, and protects and preserves the dignity of each (pg. 2).

The CWLA's *Division of Cultural Competence* encourages its members to move forward in adopting such a practice. They suggest:

Ten Things You Should Do To Promote Cultural Competence:
1. Make a commitment to expand knowledge about culture, cultural competence and the various dimensions of culture in your organization.

2. Make a commitment to develop an understanding of the various cultural groups within communities served by that of your agency.

3. Include culture and cultural competence principles in the strategic planning, policy development, program design, and service delivery process. Increase the organizational and individual understanding of how the various dimensions of culture impact the families the agency serves and the staff that works with them.

4. Be committed to promoting cultural competence. Develop this commitment through staff development and training, hiring, retention, career advancement, performance evaluations and employee policies that support culturally competent and linguistically appropriate practice.

5. Create safe, secure, supportive environments where staff can explore and develop an understanding of all cultures. Create formal partnerships with community organizations and encourage staff to actively engage communities and families in the development of policy, program design, and service delivery models.

6. Be active in local communities. Engage communities by recruiting local citizens for the Board of Directors, in voting positions, and on advisory teams and task forces. Encourage and support staff to become involved in community boards and cultural activities.

7. Be an example to tribes, communities and families that work with your agency by making hiring decisions that are reflective of the diversity of those populations. More importantly, make sure that staff has an understanding and respect for the richness, strength and additional capacity culture and diversity bring to the workplace.

8. Advocate for the development of cultural competence principles in other groups to which your agency belongs. Include criteria in Request for Proposals and other contracts that place an emphasis on the ability of the applicant, contractor, or consultant to demonstrate the capacity and ability to achieve positive results that are culturally competent and linguistically appropriate, and applicable to the needs of children and families being served.

9. Become more proactive about recognizing and resolving conflicts that can occur when differing cultures interact. Encourage staff to speak out when they recognize intolerance whether or not they are the targets.

10. If your agency provides educational and/or recreational opportunities for the community and families served, makes sure that they include experiences that are reflective of all cultural groups. For instance, many tribes and communities have museums or cultural centers that host a variety of events throughout the years and on holidays. Also, during the summer many communities have various festivals that celebrate the culture, traditions, artwork, and dance of racial and ethnic groups. Encourage children and youth to share their knowledge about the cultural groups to which they belong.

CULTURAL COMPETENCE THWARTED

The aforementioned list is one of sound principles. Putting it into agency practice is sometimes another story. To clarify this point, two examples will be related at this time. While these vignettes could have been included in the chapters on family work or ethics, they are included here because of their implications towards cultural intolerance.

The first example involves a child whom a county Department was attempting to place back with his family. Agency "A" (where the child was residing) did not agree. They felt the biological family could not provide the proper care for the child. Discussions to resolve these differences in opinion were heated. Obviously, when an agency, Department, and child's family are having a monumental dispute, tensions can run high. However, the child should never be targeted, or made a pawn in the debate.

One day in the residence this youngster was having a difficult day. He just could not stay focused, was verbally aggressive towards the other children, and was giving staff members a difficult time. (It was obvious the staff were already upset with the child's family for fighting the agency's decision that he not return home.) Finally, one of these residential workers walked over to the child pointing a finger at his chest and said, "I'm getting sick and tired of your bullshit. You better knock the bullshit off now!" The child quieted down, perhaps in fear that this staff member was losing control.

And to think the agency stated this child shouldn't move back home. Even if he did, could he have been spoken to in a more disrespectful manner than this? While it is impossible for staff members to hide their emotions all the time, to speak disrespectfully to a child demonstrates inadequate sensitivity, unacceptable communication skills, and, in this case, speaks to a lack of respect for the child and his or her family.

This incident highlights the belief that some feel a child in care is the *agency's property*. As related in chapter six, nothing could be further from the truth. Children are in residential placement because they need *temporary* shelter and treatment. In fact, today in some states, thinking of residential placement as a long term modal is archaic. We all need to change our mind set. We need to be working as a team with the state or county Department, and the child's family. Residential placements are not in operation to block family reunification. These facilities are funded to help children and their families.

The other example of intolerance involves an adolescent who was questioning his sexual orientation. When a staff member heard that the youth discussed his gender identity with his clinician he became agitated. Later, at the residence, the staff member called the young man aside and said, "You're not going to practice being gay in this house as long as I'm here."

This is yet another example of cultural insensitivity. We need to address the issue of homophobia in our field through training and developing policies that prohibit such contempt for clients. In regards to the issue of sexual orientation, workers must realize that some youth do question their sexual identity – and they have that right. These orientation questions may revolve around the fact that some boys in care were abused by other males. While program staff should be cognizant of client relationships within the milieu, and while an agency has the duty to stop the act of homosexuality between youth in care (just as they have the duty to stop acts of heterosexuality), program staff do not have the right to stop clients from discussing issues of sexual orientation.

Assessing an Agency's Practice of Cultural Competence

Today there are many ways to deal with cultural insensitivity. Ideas include:

- Training and program in-services.
- Open agency discussions.
- Partnering with community groups to institute cultural practice. In addition, accreditation is becoming more of a necessity than a philosophical discussion. As states continue to mandate that agencies become accredited, it is forcing programs to look at its services and how it provides them to the child, their family, and the larger community.

When an agency is discussing cultural competence, the CWLA (2001) recommends that the following micro-assessment be utilized for self-examination:

1. Would an accreditation entity give your organization a high rating for cultural competency?

2. Do the tribes, communities and families you serve feel that they receive culturally applicable and appropriate services that meet their needs?

3. Do your staff members feel valued, respected and appreciated?

4. If asked to rate the cultural competence of your organization, what would your clients and their families say?

CHANGING WITH THE TIMES

The times, they are a changing for sure. In 1997, to move towards a national consensus on culture and diversity, the U.S. Department of Health and Human Services, Office of Minority Health (OMIT) asked groups to review existing competence standards, and develop an agenda for future works. By 1999, *The Cultural and Linguistic Competence Standards and Research Agenda Project* was presented to OMIT. The first part of this report recommended national standards for culturally and linguistically appropriate services (CLAS). Some of the recommended standards include:

- Promoting and supporting the attitudes, behaviors, knowledge and skills necessary for staff to work respectfully and effectively with patients and each other in a culturally diverse work environment.

- Having a comprehensive management strategy to address culturally and linguistically appropriate services, including strategic goals, plans, policies, procedures, and designated staff responsible for implementation.

- Utilize formal mechanisms for community and consumer involvement in the design and execution of service delivery, including planning, policy making, operations, evaluations training and, as appropriate, treatment planning.

Ensuring cultural competence is an arduous task. Its success is predicated on a system's commitment and responsibility to the process. Cultural competence for the organization entails a set of congruent practice skills, attitudes, politics and structures that come together in a system or agency or among professionals and enable that system, that agency, or those professionals to work effectively in the context of cultural differences (Family Resource Coalition, 1996). A program that insists on a cultural competent staff is committing to best practice.

THE CHANGING FACE OF AMERICAN ETHNICITY

In 1972, 319,000 youth resided in out-of-home care. This was equal to four out of every 1,000 children living in the United States (U.S. House of Representatives, 1998). In 1974, Congress enacted the *Child Abuse and Prevention Treatment Act* (CAPTA). CAPTA gave states funding to assist them in developing child protective services. Since 1974, 250,000 additional children entered the system. By March of 2000, the number of youth in care numbered 588,000. This was an increase to 8 out of every 1,000 children in the population (U.S. Department of Health and Human Services, 2001 c).

In addition to looking at the numbers of youth in care we must also look at socioeconomics. Issues such as discrimination, substance abuse, homelessness and poverty are all intertwined in today's society, placing greater stress on the family, combating the unit's ability to cope (Freundlich, 1997). The need for assistance is at an all-time high. Yet, the available services cannot keep up with the demand. Waiting lists are long. In addition, the call that programs be cut or reduced further compounds the problem.

The remainder of the chapter will address the following areas:
a. The disproportionate number of minority children in out-of-home care versus their representation in American society.
b. How programs can respect a child's culture within the milieu.

WHAT DO THE NUMBERS TELL US ABOUT CHILDREN IN CARE?

There is no denying that children of color make up a large portion of youth in care. This can be considered to be the byproduct of the shifts and racial backgrounds of the American population (Barbell & Freundlich, 2001). While people of color currently constitute 25% of the population we have seen increases in the non-white population of our country (U.S. Census Bureau, 2001a). For example, between 1980 — 1998, the African American population increased by 25%, Native Americans and Alaskan Natives by 51%, Latinos by 107% and Asian/Pacific Islanders by 177% (U.S. Census Bureau, 1999). The numbers have similarly grown in the child welfare system. In 1980 children of color made up 43.7% of children in care. By 1999 that number had grown to nearly 61% (U.S. Department of Health and Human Services, 2000a).

What about demographics within the milieu? If we were to look at many residential programs, and judge them based on the color of staff, we would presume that most children in placement are white. In some instances this is the case. But, when we look at the number of white youth in placement versus their proportion in our society, the representation is skewed. Based upon current data we know that white children represent 65% of the population, but, they make up only 33% of children in care (U.S. States Department of Human Services, 2000a, U.S. Census Bureau, 2001b).

There is quite a contrast when we compare this to African American youth in care. These children are most disproportionately represented in our field (Barbell and Freundlich, 2001). African

American children represented 15% of the population in 1999 yet they represented 42% of the out-of-home care population (U.S. Department of Human Services, 2000a, U.S. Census Bureau, 200 lb). Over the last decade we have witnessed African American children entering the system more than any other ethnicity (Tatara, 1993).

In regards to other ethnic groups, Latino, Native American/Alaskan Native, and Asian/Pacific Islander populations are growing in this country (U.S. Census Bureau, 2000 lb). Latino children make up 9% of the population, Native American/Alaskan Native youth make up 1% of the population and Asian/Pacific Islander children make up 4% of the population. By and large these groups are proportionately represented in our system (U.S. Census Bureau, 2001 b). However, there are exceptions in certain states where we find the numbers of youth in placement to be disproportionate (Barbell and Freundlich, 2001). This can be attributed to an influx of these cultures in particular geographic regions of the country. For example, in California the number of Latino children in care rose from 20% in 1988 to over 30% in 1994, only a six-year period (Wulczyn, et al. 1997). And, in North Dakota, Native American/Alaskan Native youth comprised 34% of the children in placement. (U.S. Department of Health and Human Services, 2000b).

These numbers serve to paint a broad picture of children in the system. We are struggling as a field to recruit service providers reflective of that picture. It can be a difficult fight in some geographic areas. This is understood. What is incomprehensible is that children of color still receive differential services (Barbell & Freundlich., 2001). The one systemic issue our field must change in regards to differing services is that of family involvement. African American and Latino children are less likely to have service plans that call for parental contact than their white peers in placement (Close, 1983, Olson, 1982, Stehno, 1990 and Shyne & Schroeder, 1978).

Family and cultural involvement should be paramount in a child's treatment plan. This issue should not be up for debate. While we proclaim to be in the business of helping all children, in some cases we are unconsciously permitting racism in our field. The implications of keeping minority children away from their families can have a lasting impact on these youth. As they leave the system and enter the *real world*, who and what do they have to turn to in times of need if programs have kept them from their families and their culture. (See chapter six for more on family work.)

Making the Milieu Reflective of the Ethnic Diversity of all Children

When a youngster enters the child welfare system it does not mean that they discard their identity. Imagine if you will, an African American child entering placement. Now imagine this child being away from home for the first time. He is frightened, afraid, and very leery of adults. This is compounded when white people (only) greet him at the front door. Imagine what must be going through his mind when he looks around and sees other children of color, but all the adults are white. The child then glances at the walls. The only artwork he sees is that reflecting scenery with the white culture portrayed. Then there are issues such as meals, personal care items, etc. In this example the agency may be unwittingly recreating the visual culture of slavery.

When children lose their home it does not mean that they should lose their culture. In this day and age it is easy to make the milieu a setting sensitive to the ethnicity of all its members. A good start is in the artwork that a program (home) displays. With technology being what it is today the internet can cut through the barriers of the past. The internet alone provides thousands of resources. It offers links to a multitude of web-sites where one can purchase multicultural prints and other artwork.

When establishing an office at an agency for which I worked, one of the first things we did was log onto the internet to purchase prints by African American, Native American, Latino, and Asian artists. We wanted folks to feel that they were welcome when they came to our office. In hosting numerous trainings and meetings, we wanted our office to demonstrate that we not only respected the culture of our peers, but that we celebrated diversity.

Artwork is just a small step to creating diversity in the milieu. Another logical step would be meal preparation. With this initiative adults (again) have little research to conduct. They can simply ask the children what their favorite dinners are. They can also have youth help them shop for foods at the market and assist in the meal preparation.

If a child is unsure of the ingredients for a particular dish (as is understandable) what is wrong with consulting the child's family? (If this is not a possibility, staff can do a little research either on-line or at the library.) Food is important to a child, both physiologically and psychologically. Meals can be a way to help a youngster keep in touch with their culture. It can also be rewarding to a child's housemates, as they will experience some diversity.

This should hold true especially around the holidays. There is no reason why we can't celebrate all cultures and customs, especially through meals. During a workshop on diversity I learned of an agency that practiced such programming during the holiday season. I listened as staff enthusiastically discussed how they had weekly dinners, one night a week in December, at their different group homes. Each celebration was reflective of a different culture. This is a great idea. Not only do youth experience a variety of holiday celebrations, but also staff members and children are exposed to different customs and cultures, from Christmas to Kwanzaa to Hanukkah.

The added benefit to a holiday schedule like this is that it adds structure during a sometimes difficult period for youth in care. Many times children in residential placement experience abandonment issues during the holidays. They wonder what their families are doing, and if they will see them for the holiday (whatever theirs may be). If it is a gift-giving holiday they wonder if their family will have a present for them. Therefore celebrations like that at the aforementioned agency help the child by focusing on something other than the Christmas day celebration.

When I was a residential coordinator, the facilities celebrated what we called *Multicultural Day* each August. All the homes in the children's program brought different foods reflective of their various cultures, and, more importantly, the heritage of the children. We played games, culminating in the breaking of the piñata. The day was always something we looked forward to as we celebrated our children and the diverse cultures we as Americans are proud to call our own. Aside from an annual celebration such as this, agencies can also celebrate diversity by recognizing the following months in which various cultures celebrate their heritage:

- February: *Black History Month*
- May: *Asian Heritage Month*

- October: *Latino Heritage Month*
- November: *Native American Heritage Month*

Celebrating these months could be a time to read a book together or watch a movie that is reflective of an event or individual from that culture. Staff and children might also prepare a meal together that is reflective of the culture celebrated. The ideas are endless.

CULTURE AS IT DEFINES CHILDREN IN RESIDENTIAL PLACEMENT

Residential placement staff should get into the habit of looking at the culture of children in our care at more than *face value*. Children in residential placement are not simply culturally diverse because of nationality or color. For example, children born and raised in poverty, and neglected as a result, reflect different cultural values than others more fortunate. Kids who grow up in an abusive, profanity-riddled, fast food eating family will also present with a different set of values. These are all characteristics of culture, but in a slightly different perspective. Recognizing a child's ethnic culture is important, but recognizing his or her *values* culture is also important.

Once again we may find that this is a good place to go back to meeting the needs of children. The examples of children cited in the last paragraph may have been African-American, Latino, Asian or Caucasian. Their living environment established a definitive culture based on the conditions in which the children had to survive. The children bring with them into our programs the values (or lack thereof) that were instilled in them via their living environment.

Workers in our field have seen some of the needs lacking in these children. They also see the need to impart new (or refine) values within the child. Again, these cultural values were imparted on the child by his or her living conditions and/or environment. Examples of this are listed in the chart on page 103:

NEED	PAST CULTURAL VALUE	NEW VALUE TO INSTILL (NEED TO BE MET)
FOOD	FOOD may have been scarce. The child may have eaten an abundance of junk food that he or she had prepared. The child may not place a value in nutrition - nor experience food as a source of nurturance from adults.	A healthy diet should be imparted to children. They should learn that junk foods and fast foods are not nutritional and shouldn't be thought of as an everyday meal. In addition, youth should be taught that mealtime is very important. It is a time for people to come together
CLOTHING	Just as with the example of food, clothing may have been scarce. Children may have worn old and dirty clothing, accepting this practice. As a result it may have reaffirmed to them that they were unworthy. In addition, they may have developed feelings of guilt if new clothes were bought for them placed a strain on the family budget.	Staff should help the children pick out new clothes — and use this as an opportunity for the child to excercise self-expression, thus bolstering their self-esteem. This will show the child that they are worthy and cared for by the adults in the program. (It goes without saying that if a child is old enough, he or she should also be taught to care for their clothing, learning how to launder them.)
HEALTH CARE	Children may come into our programs having received limited to no medical care. This may have led to frequent illness, poor dental hygiene, and feelings of worthlessness.	The first thing staff have to do for a new child in placement is have their medical needs met. This includes a physical and dental examination. This may cause the child a great deal of anxiety. Staff should understand this. Once the medical treatment is completed, and the children know they will be cared for properly, they should feel better about themselves.
SHELTER	Children may have had inadequate housing with no heat. Some may have had decent housing but moved often. They also may have lived in an unsafe environment.	Staff should give new youth a tour of the home, reaffirming that the home is always heated properly, furnished and that the child will be kept safe. Children should also remain in one home in a program. They should not be moved from one home to another. Stability is very important.

This chart offers but a few suggestions for helping children meet needs and deal with cultural influences due to their past environment. The University of Oklahoma National Resource Center (1986) also makes the following suggestions when helping children in residential placement:

- *Accept children where they are.* The children's needs history is part of their ecological history, which carries with them strong values and benefits (National Resource Center, 1986). Staff will be making a big mistake if they say, "How can you mix peas with mustard?" or "Didn't your mother ever teach you how to brush your teeth properly?" Children must feel accepted as they are, and safe to be who they are, before they will be motivated to alternative behaviors (National Resource Center, 1986).

- *Teach alternative behaviors as the child is ready.* Children cannot be forced to learn something before they are ready too. As noted in earlier chapters, a child's chronological age does not always equate to their developmental and emotional stage. Modeling should occur at a low-key pace. As children become more interested in learning, staff can do more teaching.

- *Developing positive relationships with a child is the key to your role as a residential worker.* If you are not successful with a particular child, find another staff member who can be (National Resource Center, 1986).

- *Make sure your own needs are being met.* Being a residential worker requires motivation. Staff will be working with troubled children each and every day they report to work. This means that you need to come to work full of energy and enthusiasm, ready to help kids. They are not in residential placement to meet your needs. You have to make sure these needs are met yourself. Remember, you must put the needs of the children over your needs at all times (National Resource Center, 1986).

The first suggestion in this last segment is the key to working with children in our care. The culture in which many of children in residential placement have learned has not always been one that we as workers have experienced or readily accept. But, in order to be successful in our work we have to accept the children where they are. This will give us the chance to help them become more comfortable in the milieu environment. Eventually they will begin to learn new skills and strategies.

JEFFREY THE LITTLE AFRICAN-AMERICAN BOY WHO THOUGHT HE WAS ITALIAN

Jeffery was an eleven-year-old African-American boy with whom I worked with in a group home. For most of his life white people in placement had cared him for. Jeffery was an intelligent youngster and was just a joy to be around. The only problem was that he identified himself as being an Italian. This was because he was convinced he was part Italian. He was fond of the Italian meals my wife Laurie would prepare, especially hot Italian sausage. In addition, during the holidays, we would visit our families, both of whom shared strong Italian heritages. Jeffery came to love eating with our relatives as lasagna, ravioli, stuffed shells, macaroni and meatballs, and, of course, Italian sausage was on the menu.

At first it was cute to hear Jeffery tell people that he was Italian. However, it wasn't so amusing when we found out that he had little knowledge of his own heritage. This was especially disconcerting when a family expressed an interest in adopting him. (We knew that Jeffery wanted to be adopted by white people. That was understandable as all his caregivers had been white.) However, the family that wanted to adopt him was African-American. It was apparent to my wife and me that there was a big gap in his cultural identity. I don't think that he even knew the void existed.

Jeffery and I started talking about his culture. We began in the 1850's. This was a logical start since he was a Civil War buff, a common interest that he and I shared. He was very smart and enjoyed our talks on Harriet Tubman and Fredrick Douglas. We eventually worked our way up to Jackie Robinson and Martin Luther King. In addition, he loved basketball. This led to discussions about Bill Russell, and what he went through playing basketball for the Boston Celtics in the 1960's (a white community dominated by Irish-Americans, in some neighborhoods resistant to integration).

I did not bombard him with all the information I could think of at any one time. If I did, he would have seen through me. Instead, I would file information in the back of my mind as I thought about it. Sometimes my ignorance of the culture required going to the library to do some research while the kids were in school. It was not only a *labor of love*, but was also a great learning experience for myself.

Every now and then while we were shooting the basketball around, or taking a walk, I would weave Jeffery's heritage into the conversation. Other times, while things were on his mind (or after we had watched a video on Fredrick Douglas, or a documentary on the Civil Rights movement) he would ask me a multitude of questions. Sometimes this required another trip to the library, which he loved. Eventually, Jeffery would see that he had a lot to be proud of in being

African-American. When a family of color did adopt him he did not experience culture shock.

ALL OF US ARE JUST PEOPLE HELPING PEOPLE

Jefferey's story is surely but one example of how workers are helping children throughout our programs. Organizations are built by and for people (Nash, 1999). Children's residential programs have helped thousands of youth of all cultures. That is why there is hope that we can make adjustments to work with the changing face of America. Deep down, all of us are just people who want to help others. It is this author's opinion that once an organization endorses change, its proactive workforce can *move mountains*. Nash (1999) contends that the normal process of this change includes the following steps:

- A change in thinking, a new awareness and understanding, acceptance of different attitudes, beliefs, values, and perceptions;
- A change in actions accompanied by a clear and realistic plan for changing practice; and
- A change in habit as the commitment to the new way of thinking and acting increases.

Long lasting, effective change cannot occur without both individual and organizational changes in behavior (Nash, 1999). It is also the opinion of this author that we have the will to ensure such change occurs in our field now. The importance of diversity is monumental to children's residential work. Only when talk equals action will we have incorporated a treatment environment that respects both the staff members and the children that we care for.

CHAPTER EIGHT
Ethics in our Field: Do we Walk The Walk?

"That which is wrong is not the evil of bad people but the silence of good people."

Dr. Martin Luther King

THE WALLS OF SILENCE

When I was a teenager I remember seeing the movie *Serpico*. The film is the true account of Frank Serpico, the police officer that became so disgusted with the injustices of the NYPD (New York Police Department) he had to either go public or live with a guilty conscience. He had gone to the administration of the Department on numerous occasions without result. Serpico courageously chose to go to the media, breaking the *blue wall of silence*. It nearly cost him his life. In the end the NYPD was exposed, the corrupt lost their jobs, and the Department was reorganized. Serpico, himself, was never really the same. His peers could never forgive him and he eventually had to leave the NYPD. However, in an interview in 1999 I heard Serpico state that he was happy he did the right thing. In saving many innocent people from mistreatment, he had found an inner peace.

In the 1970's another *wall of silence* was shattered when Bob Woodward and Carl Bernstein, writers for the *Washington Post*, broke the story of Watergate. This led to the resignation of President Richard Nixon. While these men were not totally motivated by moral obligation as Serpico had been, those who have read *All the President's Men*, or have seen the movie of the same title, know that Woodward and Bernstein were putting their personal and professional lives on the line.

Numerous examples such as the aforementioned can be cited. America is a better place because many brave individuals have chosen to take a stand against a multitude of injustices. Though we still have much work to do, our country is making progress on issues of discrimination and gender. Maybe one day our country will even take actions to stabilize the gap between the *haves* and *have-nots*. To further this progress we must be willing to *see* injustices, cite them, and listen to the message without persecuting the messenger.

The field of children's residential programming is no different than any other profession. We have our own issues and problems. Some agencies may unwittingly put up their own walls to prevent others from seeing what's happening inside their programs. And sadly, we have some people who do not consider core values and high ethical standards as important virtues. All this holds true in spite of the fact that we are a human service profession, charged with helping wounded children.

OUR WALLS OF SILENCE

In 1990, *Covenant House,* a famous New York site for homeless and runaway teenagers, was rocked with "one of the most widely publicized scandals in the history of 20th century American youth work" (Youth Today, 2000). Its founder, Father Bruce Ritter, resigned in February of that year amidst charges of his sexually preying on the teen boys that his program sheltered. He denied the charges. The rest of the *Covenant House* leadership worked alongside him in covering up the evidence. They referred to the four boys who alleged the abuse as "liars." Subsequent to Fr. Ritter's resignation, 116 boys had come forward with their own stories of Ritter's sexual assaults on them (Youth Today, 2000).

Unfortunately, this is not an isolated incident. Our work is not devoid of sexual predators and deviants. It is also not free from those who would cover up such incidents. Until that day comes, we are open to any charges or accusations that the public can provide. In some cases, we deserve it.

By no means is this chapter intended to damn the field. Instead, it proposes to help all agencies move towards common values and goals in children's treatment. Our programs provide a much needed service to society. I could go on and on discussing the many fine programs helping children in my home state of Rhode Island alone. The majority of residential programs provide quality services for our nation's most vulnerable children.

These few pages are intended to help the profession focus on issues that we need to address. Instead of pretending that our field has no problems, and discarding things that we know are wrong, I have chosen to look at some of our problems, some of our walls. It is too easy to say "Be quiet; our communities already have a negative opinion of group homes", or, "If people find out about this, we'll be out of business and you'll be out of a job." These warnings serve only to allow problems to persist, uncorrected. How can we say we know how to help children face their issues, if we can't face our own? We have preached to the choir for so long now that some of us may have actually forgotten our responsibilities.

The belief that *our field is continually questioned so silence might actually be golden* is a polarized misconception. It ought to be dismissed. Our work should be questioned when things go wrong. Most residential programs receive their funds from the local and/or federal government. We should want to be held accountable. Communities are right to do so.

Our field must be prepared for public accountability. For centuries, the conduct of societies' most trusted servants was deemed beyond reproach. Today such blind faith is disappearing from the landscape. (Peterson, 1992) Whether we in children's residential programs want to admit it or not, we are quasi "public servants." Not only must we be accountable, but also, we must accept the responsibility for helping shape a brighter future. While we can feign responsibility there is no way to dismiss accountability.

The majority of agencies do understand the vital role they play. They understand that children in residential placement need specific treatment and special care. These workers know that they are not simply glorified babysitters. Their agencies have strong policies, excellent training for staff and promote "teamwork" within their facilities. The most successful agencies keep the child (and their family's) treatment as the focal point.

It is easy for youth to be re-victimized within residential placement, especially when two factors are realized: 1) The children in treatment are often very vulnerable; and 2) The low pay scale for direct care workers creates high staff turnover rates. This allows some inappropriate workers to "slip through the cracks".

Grant Charles, Heather Coleman and Jane Matheson (1993) sum up the potential for re-victimization when considering the aforementioned factors. They conclude:

The children who are most traumatized often end up in residential programming.

These centers have the potential to offer young children powerful assistance in the healing process. Unfortunately, the centers can also be the site of further exploitation and harm (p.20).

Regrettably, it might be inevitable that a percentage of children will be exploited and/or victimized while in placement. Even the best programs face this issue. However, agencies can play a more proactive role in minimizing the potential for institutional abuse. Charles, Coleman and Matheson (1993) note, "Agencies within which the staff feel disempowered or maltreated by the administration or that have poorly developed hiring procedures have higher suspected rates of abuse." (p.19)

One True Story

In the mid-1990's "Joe Smith" was working as a direct care staff member at a residential program. After four years on the job an issue of enormous proportion confronted him. It was apparent that a child was being abused or neglected at a group home within this program. In addition to staff hunches, the child in question was pleading for help, as were his peers. Joe's co-workers were instructed that they could not talk about the issue, but they still discussed it when they were out of earshot of the administration team. Folks did not know what to do and felt helpless. They feared for the children still under the care of the accused worker.

Like all matters covered with secrecy, staff continued to talk. The problem on the agency end was that while the administration could discuss some details, an individual worker (alleged to have committed abuse or neglect) has the right to keep his/her name from being disclosed until something has been substantiated. In this profession, once a staff member is accused of abuse they are forever guilty in the eyes of some. Their name will be tainted. That is why the issue the agency faced was delicate at best.

The problem was that the administration did not want to state anything. In fact, they did not even want to discuss the child's well being. This may have been the wrong way to handle the situation, especially after it was known that the accused perpetrator was still working with the child. This staff member could have been put on administrative leave – or been given another assignment until the matter was investigated. If the administration would have made it clear that the child in question was now safe and his needs were being met, the matter might have been resolved. But, that didn't happen and staff started to wonder "why" aloud. Soon the administration began to seek out those who were talking and warned them "to stop the grapevine."

Within a half-year of this incident Joe was promoted to supervisor. He thought he could finally resolve this issue and stop the internal under currents that were perpetuating the problem. He still could not get answers. In fact, things became even worse. At an administrative meeting Joe was told that if a particular staff member could not drop the incident (stop talking about the safety of the child making the accusation) he should be fired. People were panicked and wanted the issue to end – even if they had to close it themselves.

It also did not make things better when Joe cooperated with those investigating the case. It was the right thing to do but yielded detrimental results. The investigators told the agency all that Joe had told them, and the agency's director was provided copies of all notes made in their discussions with Joe. By the time the investigation was over, Joe was ostracized and his time at this agency was borrowed. He would not be invited to administrative meetings, he and his staff were always under the microscope, and a financial raise "was hard to come by." This in spite of the fact that the residential team working at the agency was performing admirably.

Joe didn't know what happened during this investigation. Did those investigating the case miss something? He didn't know. All he knows now is that he was labeled as the bad guy because he did his job. Suspected child abuse should be reported. Failure to report it is the real offense. In Joe's case and in many others, the messenger becomes the *bad person* targeted by their agency, and in most states this is against the law. The message being discarded is the real offense. It is a problem that our field cannot pretend does not exist.

Even after years have passed Joe feels he was unfairly labeled a traitor by the agency he gave years of devoted labor to. But he knows he did the right thing in spite of the system failing. In the end, the person who committed the abuse has been punished and the child being abused was moved to another agency. Strangely enough, Joe believes most of the people involved in the agency's handling of this case are good people; good people who committed very bad actions. In trying to understand how a child was allowed to be abused in the residential placement, Joe believes that fear and confusion were the motivating factors behind the agency's improper response.

Some may argue that fear and confusion are not justifiable excuses for what transpired at this agency. We may be tempted to say that the reporting laws are very clear. This may be true, but remember: human beings enforce laws and sometimes this leads to differing interpretations of what is right. While some investigations lead to stiff sanctions or the closing of a program, the same system allows greater leniency towards other agencies. We should be establishing a practice whereby all agencies are held to the same high standards. There should never be exceptions when a child has been harmed in residential placement.

FEAR + CONFUSION = COVER UPS?

In some instances it is easy to understand an agency's fear and confusion when a child is abused in their program. This is especially true if it is the program's first incident. It is difficult for some to admit that something bad actually happened in their agency.

Robert Bloom (1993) acknowledges that the fear of reporting is not uncommon in cases of institutional negligence. Agencies may fear the consequences if they report, so some choose not to disclose the facts. Others fail to believe, or do not want to believe that a child would be harmed in their facility. Bloom relates, "It has been this author's uniform experience that allegations of abuse of residents by staff members are true" (Bloom, 1993, p. 92). He also urges agencies to listen to any allegation non-defensively. This may help the agency to face the facts and avoid building a wall of silence.

Robert Bloom is a noted professional in the issues of neglect and abuse in residential facilities. He has experience with many cases regarding institutional neglect and abuse. In the later part of the 1980's, he researched specific cases with the state of Illinois. Bloom, Denton and Caflish (1991) looked at data provided by the Illinois Department of Children, Youth and Families. They discovered 211 allegations of institutional childhood sexual abuse were reported between 1987-1991. Of these, 57 (27%) were substantiated after investigation. That means that one out of every four allegations of abuse was verified. What about all the incidents that go unreported?

And, what about all those calls not deemed worthy of an investigation?

As a professional taking his duty to report suspected abuse very seriously, I myself had made calls to the Child Protective Agency in my state when I was a residential worker. Many of these calls were not investigated. Once when I tried to get the name of the person taking a report, I was unsuccessful. I remember saying to this individual, who stated a particular call would not warrant an investigation, "I didn't get your name." The gentlemen answered "That's because I didn't give it to you." End of conversation.

ETHICAL CODES IN THE CHILD CARE PROFESSION

The aforementioned incidents and data demonstrate that our work is in need of professional standards. Though we are in the helping profession, and it would seem that we would be more cognizant of treating others fairly and decently, we must find a code of ethics pertinent to our field. Today, we have such a code being promoted by the *Association of Child and Youth Care Practices*' North American Child and Youth Care initiative. It is a work in progress and gives our field something to look towards.

Characteristics of a profession are a systemic body of theory, professional authority, sanction of the community, a regulative code of ethics and a professional culture (Greenwood, 1957). This premise is the focal point in the introduction to the aforementioned code of ethics. The code is included in this text to help us focus on our work as a profession.

CODE OF ETHICS
STANDARDS FOR PRACTICE OF NORTH AMERICAN CHILD AND YOUTH CARE PROFESSIONALS

PRINCIPLES AND STANDARDS

I. RESPONSIBILITY FOR SELF:

A. Maintains competency.

   1. Takes responsibility for identifying, developing, and fully utilizingknowledge and abilities for professional practice.

   2. Obtains training, education, supervision, experience and/or counsel to assure competent service.

B. Maintains high standards of professional conduct.

C. Maintains physical and emotional well-being.

   1. Aware of own values and their implication for practice.
   2. Aware of self as a growing and strengthening professional.

II. RESPONSIBILITY TO THE CLIENT
(Client is defined as the child, family, and former clients)

A. Above all, shall not harm the child, youth or family.

   1. Does not participate in practices that are disrespectful, degrading, dangerous, exploitive intimidating, psychologically damaging, or physically harmful to clients.

B. Provides expertise and protection.

   1. Recognizes, respects, and advocates for the rights of the child, youth and family.

C. **Recognizes that professional responsibility is to the client and advocates for the client's best interest.**

D. **Ensures services are sensitive to and non-discriminatory of clients regardless of race, color, ethnicity, national origin, national ancestry, age, gender, sexual orientation, marital status, religion, abilities, mental or physical handicap, medical condition, political belief, political affiliation, socioeconomic status.**

   1. Obtains training, education, supervision, experience, and/or counsel to assure competent service.

E. **Recognizes and respects the expectations and life patterns of clients.**
   1. Designs individualized programs of child, youth and family care to determine and help meet the psychological, physical, social, cultural and spiritual needs of the clients.

   2. Designs programs of child, youth, and family care which address the child's developmental status, understanding, capacity, and age.

F. **Recognizes that there are differences in the needs of children, youth and families.**

   1. Meets each client's needs on an individual basis.

   2. Considers the implications of acceptance for the child, other children, and the family when gratuities or benefits are offered from a child, youth or family.

G. **Recognizes that competent service often requires collaboration. Such service is a cooperative effort drawing upon the expertise of many.**

   1. Administers medication prescribed by lawful prescribing practitioner in accordance with prescribed directions and

only for medical purposes. Seeks consultation when necessary.

   2. Refers the client to other professionals and/or seeks assistance to ensure appropriate services.

   3. Observes, assesses, and evaluates services/treatments prescribed or designed by other professionals.

H. Recognizes the client's membership within a family and community, and facilitates the participation of significant others in service to the client.

I. Fosters client self-determination.

J. Respects the privacy of clients and holds in confidence information obtained in the course of professional service.

K. Ensures that the boundaries between professional and personal relationships with clients is explicitly understood and respected, and that the practitioner's behavior is appropriate to this difference.

   1. Sexual intimacy with a client, or the family member of a client, is unethical.

III.   RESPONSIBILITY TO THE EMPLOYER/EMPLOYING ORGANIZATION:

A. Treats colleagues with respect, courtesy, fairness, and good faith.

B. Relates to the clients of colleagues with professional consideration.

C. Respects the commitments made to the employer/employing organization.

IV. RESPONSIBILITY TO THE PROFESSION:

A. Recognizes that in situations of professional practice the standards in this code shall guide the resolution of ethical conflicts.

B. Promotes ethical conduct by members of the profession.

    1. Seeks arbitration or mediation when conflicts with colleagues require consultation and if an informal resolution seems appropriate.

    2. Reports ethical violations to appropriate persons and/or bodies when an informal resolution is not appropriate.

C. Encourages collaborative participation by professionals, client, family and community to share responsibility for client outcomes.

D. Ensures that research is designed, conducted, and reported in accordance with high quality Child and Youth Care practice, and recognized standards of scholarship, and research ethics.

E. Ensures that education and training programs are competently designed/delivered.

    1. Programs meet the requirements/claims set forth by the program.

    2. Experiences provided are properly supervised.

F. Ensures that administrators and supervisors lead programs in high quality and ethical practice in relation to clients, staff, governing bodies, and the community.

1. Provides support for professional growth.

2. Evaluates staff on the basis of performance on established requirements.

V. <u>RESPONSIBILITY TO SOCIETY</u>:

A. Contributes to the profession in making services available to the public.

B. Promotes understanding and facilitates acceptance of diversity in society.

C. Demonstrates the standards of this Code with students and volunteers.

D. Encourages informed participation by the public in shaping social policies and institutions.

ETHICS IN THE AGENCY AND CHILDREN'S RIGHTS

There is a movement to have this code of ethics accepted nationally. This would be a step in the right direction. However, each residential placement agency is expected to have standards that the child and staff abide by. It is a two way street. If the clients are expected to conduct themselves in a certain way, the staff members must model appropriate behavior. This includes our language, the clothes we wear into work, and our respect for others. We cannot expect the children to follow the rules of the milieu if we feel they do not apply to staff. This extends to even the following basic activities within the milieu:
- Staff and children should eat the same meals – together at the dinner table.
- The residence should be clean at all times.
- Staff and children should decide on group activities, television shows, etc.

- Children should have input in room arrangements, re-arrangements.

Perhaps one of the most difficult things for some staff members to remember is that children in care have rights regardless of their behavior. Sure, they all have issues, and discipline is sometimes required. However, children do not go into residential treatment to be punished. Instead, they arrive at our doors for care. Some of their basic rights (and in Rhode Island they are pursuant to General Law 42-72-15) are:

- Basic needs such as food, clothing, shelter and personal belongings.
- To be treated with respect and dignity.
- To contact family and friends by phone, mail and/or visits unless there are reasons to stop this due to treatment or safety.
- To receive mail.
- To have visitors.
- To go to school.
- To practice their religion.

When we look at the aforementioned list (and children in care have many other rights) some of the items are cause for agency debate. This is a good thing. Open communication helps our profession. The more we can talk about what is right and what is wrong, the better our chances for establishing just standards.

The following are examples for consideration. They are issues that staff members in residential placement have had to deal with on a daily basis.

Mail: Johnny Jones, a resident in a group home, received mail from a classmate in the agency's school program. Residential staff members were leery of this mail as the two boys had been acting suspiciously. Their apprehension was that the letter might contain contraband. They opened the mail and found it was just a harmless card wishing Johnny a happy birthday. <u>Violation of Rights?</u> Yes. <u>What was a better staff choice?</u> Johnny could have opened the mail in front of staff. It could have also been brought into school the next day. Then, while in the presence of his clinician, Johnny could have opened the letter. If contraband were in the note it would have been discovered.

Religion: Kenny Smith had been attending church every Sunday with a staff member from his residence. Kenny loved church. One Sunday he heard the priest say that he was in the need of acolytes. Kenny asked if he could serve. The staff member referred the question to his clinician. She decided that Kenny could not serve because his family was not of the religious denomination of this particular church. When it was pointed out that his family's rights had been terminated the clinician stated that Kenny's adoptive family (whenever one was identified) might object. <u>Violation of Rights?</u> Not really. <u>Why?</u> Kenny has the right to practice a religion of his choice. In attending mass each week he was provided that right. The clinician's concern about an adoptive family that didn't exist was not justified. Still, his rights were not violated.

Chuck's Allowance: Chuck was a teenager in a residential program. He had been depositing his allowance in a savings account for just over a year. It had reached well over $300. One day his parents called Chuck's clinician and said they needed money. The clinician called the residence and told staff to take Chuck to the bank, have him withdraw his money, and have Chuck give it to his parents when they arrived at the milieu. The staff member said he didn't fell comfortable doing this, especially since Chuck was objecting to the request. The worker was ordered to take him anyway. The staff member was then called back and told to drive Chuck to his parent's house (forty minutes away), as they didn't have the money for gas. <u>Violation of Rights?</u> It could be argued to have been a violation of rights as Chuck did not want to withdraw the money he worked so hard to save. (It also seemed to cross ethical lines as the child, and staff, were ordered to do something against their will.) <u>What else could have been done?</u> The clinician could have had Chuck's parents ask him if they could <u>borrow</u> the money. There would have been a value in this incident if: 1) Chuck had been asked to consider helping out his parents, and, 2) the parents realized an obligation to pay their son back for the money they borrowed. That didn't happen. As it turned out, Chuck lost some hard earned money he had saved. He also was angry at residential staff and gave them a hard time about doing chores in the future.

Telephone Calls: Clark had just been placed in a group home while his mother put her life back in order. The plan was to help mom work on her parenting skills and Clark would work on his issues. Residential staff was informed by the agency that Clark could not receive phone calls from his mother for a period of six weeks after intake. <u>Violation of Rights?</u> Yes. <u>Why?</u> Agencies cannot mandate that a family and child have no contact. In this case, the goal was for Clark to be reunified with his mother. Agencies do not have the exclusive right to prohibit calls. Some programs feel that residents need to become acclimated to the program, and that family contact will prohibit this from occurring. This is a detrimental practice to engage in. While, at times, there are treatment issues that may result in limitations on phone calls, staff cannot stop calls just because a youth is on restriction, didn't finish his or her supper, is doing their chores, etc.

Tommy's Eye: Tommy was a student attending an agency's day program. One day he began complaining his eye was bothering him. In the interim he was sent to take a time-out for speaking out on numerous occasions during a lesson. While on his way to the time-out area, Tommy insisted his eye still hurt. When the nurse happened to wander by he told her about it. She wanted to help but never had the chance. A staff member told her "Tommy is in time-out." <u>Violation of Rights?</u> Aside from a right's violation, the program's actions (rather, inactions) could be considered to border on medical neglect. <u>Why?</u> A child should never be deprived of medical attention. This is not to assume that children will not feign an illness to get out of a consequence. But, why didn't the program have the nurse take a few minutes to examine Tommy's eye? What if he was telling the truth? A child's well being is never held hostage by their behavior. Staff members are not the jury as to whether a child is in pain or not. It comes down to common sense. (If your biological child were complaining of an eye ailment would you say "Be quiet, you were told you had to take a time-out for pushing your sister.")

There are bound to be "gray areas" when it comes to interpreting violations of rights. In the aforementioned examples other professionals may have different thoughts on whether Johnny, Kenny, Chuck, Clark, and/or Tommy actually had their rights violated. That it is why an agency should have occasional discussions (as a team) regarding children's liberties and other ethical dilemmas. Programs should also have a copy of their state's *Bill of Rights* posted in each residence. Upon intake the child's clinician or house manager should review these rights with them. The greatest harm regarding a youngster's liberties is when the youth is kept out of any decision. This was evident in all four examples. When this occurs an agency is on the path to violating a child's rights.

ACCEPTING THAT CHILDREN HAVE THE RIGHT TO BE LOVED

Like many Americans in March of 2002 I saw a special on Rosie O'Donnell and the notion of children waiting to be adopted. The premise of the show was the state of Florida's practice of prohibiting youth in care from being adopted by gay couples. The irony is that so many children want to be part of loving families. This show featured segments identifying youth in loving homes wherein the caretakers happened to be gay. The flipside was all the children being abused in foster homes. Ms. O'Donnell must be given credit for bringing this injustice to light. We have come to accept a malicious practice in this country. This is that children in care can be treated in any way a foster parent (or program) chooses to treat them.

As America looks at the violations in foster homes it might not be long before the country looks at what is occurring in some highly priced residential placement programs. While the majority of these programs provide outstanding care, the few that are not will serve to handicap us all. In some cases we have lost focus of the fact that we care for young precious human beings. Does anyone really think if these kids had the choice they would choose to have been abused or mistreated, pulled from their homes, and then placed in residential care? Then, on top of that, does anyone think these children like the lack of respect some workers show? Agencies that de-humanize the face of their clients are actually worse for a child than leaving him or her in a home where they were not being properly cared for.

Final Thought on Ethics in Our Field

Taking the moral high road is not always easy to do. The path is sometimes obstructed by those who place no value in ethical conduct, and those who feel that the wrong doings in our field should be safeguarded. Residential workers are sometimes caught in this vicious circle. The important thing to do is to remember that the well being of children is affected by any "wrongs" that an individual or individuals do. Whenever a worker has doubts about the ethics of a particular practice they should ask themselves:

- Does this practice violate a child's rights?
- Does this practice deviate from the program model?
- Does this practice contradict the *Code of Ethics* set forth by the (ACYCP) North American Child and Youth Care Practitioner Initiative?

If the answer is "yes" to any of these questions the worker should probably bring the matter to their supervisor. Remember, if you feel uncomfortable carrying out a task it is your responsibility (on behalf of the child) to question the practice.

This chapter has stated some difficult things about our field. It is not a condemnation, but, rather, a suggestion for internal introspection. We are attempting to professionalize our field after all. It would seem that a step towards professionalism is adopting a *Code of Ethics*. This would bring uniformity among practice, and set an ethical standard that our field sorely needs. We have many hard-working individuals in our programs. Like any other vocation, we also have those who don't share our dedication. They are just passing through. A *Code of Ethics* sets the bar for our work. We are then in a position to raise it.

CHAPTER NINE
The Workforce Crisis

"There is more in us than we know. If we can be made to see it, perhaps for the rest of our lives, we will be unwilling to settle for anything less."
Kurt Hahn

There is no doubting the workforce crisis that has overtaken our field. In fact, it has held us in its grasp for some time now. Direct care workers are grossly underpaid, work endless shifts, receive little training, and are leaving our programs on a daily basis. It is an endless cycle that has such a detrimental impact on children in residential placement. This instability tends to recreate that of the home from which the child was removed in the first place.

We in the field acknowledge these facts and have been stating the same things for years. We are constantly reminded it is a money issue. All we need to do is raise direct care salaries and our problems will be solved. But, when looking at the problem of high turnover rates in direct care positions more closely, many professionals wonder. Is this issue solely a problem of limited resources? While raising salaries is vital, are there other things our field could be doing to make direct care positions more desirable?

Sally Smith, started as a direct care worker and can remember the things that she loved and hated about the job. Money was not the issue. She was paid a fair wage by her agency and benefits were good. (This may not always be the case at other agencies.) She loved working with the kids, the teachers who worked at the day program, the supervisors, and some members of the clinical team. What bothered her was the *ranking order* that placed direct care staff workers on the bottom of the agency totem pole. Even though, as highlighted in chapter two, there has to be an agency hierarchy, what Sally resented was the great divergence between her position and those *above* her. In spite of the fact that the direct care workers were the primary caretakers for the children, it was the clinicians and administrators that received all the *perks*. (While some clinicians were great to work with and visited children in the milieu, others were not as invested. Some could not give directions to the home the client lived in, how the house was arranged, or even the color of the child's bedroom.) Yet it was these folks who went to conferences, had the ultimate say in the child's treatment, had evenings, weekends and holidays off, and earned larger salaries. Talk about creating an unequal and undesirable work environment.

Would an increase in salary alone make a direct care worker want to stay for an extended period of time under such conditions? The shame of this practice was that there were good clinicians who could have had a greater impact within the program if they would have taken the next step (being more of a presence in the milieu). While Sally doesn't know if the agency still engages in the aforementioned practice, she does know that if there was more of a unified team at this program the direct care staff (in addition to the children) would have had felt more supported. And, support is crucial.

In addition, our field must take a more proactive approach in dealing with the rising direct care staff turnover rates. Money should be viewed as only a start. We need to invest time in initiatives that professionalize residential work. Therefore, our approach should include creating staff development opportunities for direct care workers and treating them as equal members of the team. (Though this sentiment has been repeated in this text, it can't be stressed enough.) In addition, we need to find more proactive ways in which to access money. Pleading solely to our state legislatures is not a good strategic plan.

Don't Fear the Future

There is a tendency, especially amongst smaller agencies, to be leery of new and innovative ideas. The concepts of *networking* and *accreditation* tend to be viewed with trepidation and fear. However, the times are changing, and contrary to what the cynics among us may say, the future is not about to crash upon us like an out of control tidal wave. Many professionals in our field are excited about what the future might hold. Most of us do not buy into the doom and gloom that others project. We are optimists that try to keep a hopeful view of the future. Just because something is new or just because an initiative has failed in the past, it does not mean that all things will fail. Furthermore, we live in times of shrinking budgets so we have to be open to new ideas.

We have all heard folks say, "That will never work", or "I'll believe that when I see it happen," or "Hey, we've all heard this before." These statements are made by different people for different reasons. Maybe they are stated by the administrator who doesn't want to change with the times for fear his or her budget will shrink. Maybe it is the small agency director who fears being taken over by a larger group. Or, maybe it is the cynic who just whines and complains about any type of progress, so certain in their assumption that change is never good. In many instances they are trying to get other people to go along with them. They reason that if enough agencies rebel, change will never come to fruition.

Not all change is bad. And, not all people are resistant to new ways of thinking.

Sometimes a leap of faith is all it takes. In my home state of Rhode Island, we tackled doubt and trepidation when a group of children's residential providers came together to form a third continuum of care network in the state. These were groups who had either not been invited into the first networks or were originally leery of the notion. Just listening to the discussions and planning phases has been invigorating. It shows that if programs can become more global in their thinking, and accepting of new ideas and ways to provide services to children and families, our agencies can continue to make significant contributions to society.

Rhode Island is attempting to make strides in services that focus on the child, family and the community in which they reside. In 2002, the state issued an RFP (Request for Proposals) for an in-state regional network of (accredited) agencies. This would be the second network to be funded by the state. Nationally, things are moving towards the direction of *networking* and *accreditation*. Both concepts help us in efforts to professionalize our field, move in more proactive circles, and secure a more permanent funding base for the agencies involved in the network.

Networks are important – especially for the small agencies. By joining other groups in a network formation, there is the potential for greater staff development opportunities. There is also the chance that smaller agencies could *come up to par* with the larger agencies in their network in terms of staff salaries and benefits. These are two issues (salary and benefits) that small agencies often feel handicap them. In this light, networking would actually help these programs, not to mention the sharing of other agency resources, such as philosophy, behavior management models, etc.

RI INITIATIVES TO RAISE PROGRAM BUDGETS AND PROFESSIONALIZE THE FIELD

During the State's 2000 legislative session, I had drafted a bill to help ensure rate increases for children's residential providers. Prior to this, these providers had been flat-funded for eight of twelve years in Rhode Island. Though the final version of the bill was modified, the legislation that passed called for 5% budget increases to contracted providers in FY' 2001 and 2002. The legislature also stipulated that in spite of an agency's entire budget being increased by 5%, the funds had to go to direct care staff (salaries, health insurance and benefits, and training).

In July 2001, children's residential providers were polled to ascertain the impact of the budget increase for the first year. The findings were predictable: starting salaries went up to an average of just under $21,000 while staff turnover rates decreased by nearly 10%. However, with this turnover rate still above 35%, we have a long way to go in Rhode Island. When 4 out of every 10 direct care staff workers are leaving their positions at a steady pace, it continues to create great instability within the milieu. In 2002 providers received their 5% overall contract increase per the legislation. In addition, they received an additional 3.8% for the direct care staff portion of the budget. As of the spring of 2002, turnover rates were still hovering above 30%. It seemed that the legislation was a good start, but it was not the *cure all*.

Between 1998 – 2002, Rhode Island providers had been afforded rate increases in four out of five years. In spite of this there has to be some caution. Advocates have to be careful in these endeavors as being perceived as "that group who always comes to the State House to cry over money." It is true that increases are needed to sustain quality programming. Still, there are other things that agencies could be doing to advance their cause.

One of the things that agencies can focus on is accreditation. This is important because it allows the state or county to recoup funds for agencies providing clinical services to youth under 21, and who are accredited by recognized bodies: JCACHO, COA or CARF. The good thing about the accreditation process is that it can start out as a collaborative effort. This is especially true if the collaboration involves agencies that want to form a network. Using my home state of Rhode Island as an example again, in 2000 six providers came together to work towards accreditation. In the fall of 2002 these providers received disks with generic policies that were developed together and in consultation with accreditation manuals. Agencies will be able to take the disks, tailor them to their specific programs, and then apply for accreditation. These programs will then join the handful of other agencies already accredited in the state.

Staff Development, Certification and Conferences

When I was an administrator for a residential program I once had a staff member tell me, "If you can't give me an increase (salary) this year, at least let me attend some trainings." This was more than a fair trade-off. Direct care workers need training and the ability to attend conferences as much, if not more, than any other worker within the agency. The only thing more unfortunate than an underpaid direct care worker is one who does not receive the proper training. This is a real problem in our field.

Once again I will refer to what is occurring in Rhode Island to cite the proactive stance that many states and counties are taking regarding staff development.

In 2000, a program was developed in Rhode Island (certification training) to address the lack of training for staff that work in children's residential programs. The primary focus is training direct care staff members, but the program also provides certification for supervisors and clinicians. Each of the sessions focuses on residential treatment, with specific attention paid to what care is like from the child's perspective. The content for each of the courses was designed based on surveys that were completed by residential providers. In addition, the training is refined based upon the evaluations we receive after each session.

Direct care trainings are held one day a week, for four weeks, from 8:30 am – 12:30 pm. The last week of the session concludes with a test of the material. (Staff must pass this test in order to receive their certification card.) This schedule affords workers the opportunity to attend classes when the youth in their charge are attending school. The basic training schedule for direct care certification is as follows:

Week One: *Milieu Therapy*
Week Two: *Child & Adolescent Stage Development*
Behavior Management
Week Three: *Psychotropic Medication*
Separation & Loss Issues for Children in Residential Care
Week Four: *Ethical Issues*
Managing Diversity in the Milieu

In the first year, 144 direct care workers were certified. The evaluations completed by these participants expressed an overwhelming approval of the program. The certification has been such a success, that in November 2000 the *Community College of Rhode Island* (CCRI) began collaborating with the provider community to design a certificate curriculum in Children's Residential Programming. The curriculum was finalized in June of 2002. To make it easier and less intimidating for staff to go back to school, the following initiatives were established:

- Hosting some of the first classes off campus.
- Utilizing the state's local interconnect channel to offer classes on television.
- Identifying funding to subsidize the tuition costs.

What is good about this curriculum is that completion of the thirty-credit program serves as the halfway mark towards an Associates Degree in Human Services. In addition, those staff members that have completed the aforementioned certification training course for direct care staff will have earned three (3) credits at CCRI for the course *Introduction to Children's Residential Programming*. Moreover, those who have worked in the field for a minimum of five (5) years, will earn an additional three (3) credits towards *Human Services Practicum I*. And lastly, if folks have taken any of the other courses in the past (even at some other state colleges), those credits will apply. The certificate in Children's Residential Programming consists of the following courses:

- *Introduction to Children's Residential Programming*
- *General Psychology*

- *Technical Writing*
- *Orientation to Human Services*
- *Parent and Child Relations*
- *Human Services Practicum I*
- *Guiding Children's Behavior*
- *Characteristics and Needs of Special Populations*
- *Child Growth and Development*
- *One Elective from the Human Services or Psychology departments*

This curriculum was designed to provide a well-rounded education for those working with children. The program also offers courses that will help workers with other tasks. For example, *Technical Writing* will help individuals with the day-to-day paperwork that comes with their job, such as completing incident reports, journals, filling out point charts, etc. It was important to those who worked on this curriculum that the course work not only be pertinent to working directly with youth but also the direct care position as a whole.

The last thing about the CCRI Certificate to note is that once individuals enroll in a class they are students of the college. While a good deal of time went into designing the course and making it *field friendly*, individuals will be bound by college policy. To pass each course, the student must receive a grade of "C" or higher. They must also attend the classes. The college is not bound to the practice of excusing folks from class because there was a crisis in the milieu. And, while the state is assisting with the tuition costs, there must be some investment on the individual's part. The worker must want to go back to school and take the classes.

In addition to the CCRI Certificate and certification-training programs, there is also an annual two-day conference held each year in Newport, RI. This is a very special event that focuses on residential work, offering sessions that bring direct care workers, supervisors, clinicians and administrators together. And, once in Newport, it is repeatedly stressed that our work as a team is what helps children in placement. By keeping registration costs minimal, the conference attracts some 400-500 participants each year. Sixty percent (60%) of attendees are direct care workers.

This Annual Conference was established to give direct care workers an "executive-type" conference, complete with noted speakers, fine food, and stylish settings. Sites chosen have included water views, immaculate décor, modern amenities, and four-five star ratings. Meals have included steak, swordfish, and salmon. Post-conference events have included receptions or a cruise. These efforts are appreciated and are paying off. Many residential placement staff (from direct care to clinicians to administrators) attest that the conference is one of the highlights of the year. Direct care workers deserve events like this.

How do we Bring a Team Approach To Residential Placement?

While many journal articles and other publications point to the importance of teamwork to benefit children in care, unless individual agencies subscribe to this theory, it will never become universal practice. We have grown too accustomed to a model that (in many instances) keeps residential staff in the milieu, clinicians in offices working "traditional" hours, and administrators on the sidelines. This practice is not good for kids in care and should be modified.

Our field has to want more for its direct care workers. These folks must feel like a part of a team. Three possible solutions are noted below. The first two suggestions were highlighted in other parts of the text. They are included here because of their importance.

Team meetings can't occur without all members of the team present. There are quite a few agencies that subscribe to this principle. They are programs that stress unity. It is no wonder children and youth in these settings thrive. They have the benefit of all agency employees being on the same page. Simply put, at these agencies, if a clinician wants to discuss a treatment issue, members of the residential team must be present. No residential staff present, no meeting. It's as simple as that. Why would an agency want to have a meeting on a child in residential without the input from those who spend the most time with that youngster?

Staff supervision should regularly occur. This is meant to be the actual office-time supervision of staff. As a supervisor, I always made sure each direct care worker received individual and group (with other shift members) supervision at least twice a month. These were structured meetings — not just some hodge-podge session put together when I had the time. In addition, we held weekly staff meetings, inviting clinicians and members of the administrative team to join us.

View training as a necessity for direct care staff. We have repeatedly heard that it is impossible to send direct care staff to training. The main reason used is that these workers have to be back from a training in time to cover their shift. (Where is it written of clinicians and administrators that: *thou shall not cover a shift in the milieu?*) The contradiction in this is that while clinicians' work time can be freed to attend a training or conference, even if it means missing a therapy session with a child, a line worker can't miss a shift to attend the same. (To be fair, there are countless examples of agencies where clinicians and supervisors gladly cover shifts to accommodate direct care staff attending training. Then again, these programs should be part of the norm, not the exception.)

There are plenty of agencies that subscribe to the importance of training direct care staff, and others could look to these programs for guidance on the matter. In fact, last year one executive director told me that he had to freeze all trainings due to funding issues. Prior to this decision, he had scheduled himself to attend a conference out-of-state. Once he decided that he couldn't send his staff to trainings, he cancelled his plans to attend a national conference. How many of us would like to work for such a director. This kind of leadership, that is respectful of all staff, goes a long way in creating unity.

WHERE DO WE GO FROM HERE?

One of the keys to solving the direct care crisis is for agencies to commit themselves to new thinking. We need to be more proactive and creative. The first thing we need to do is look at the obvious. I have sat on many committees attempting to make things better in the field of children's residential programming. What I have noticed is that the committees were made up of a large number of executives. While this is good, I often wonder why only directors are present. I have yet to see an actual direct care worker sit on one of these committees. While we administrators can state what we believe the problems to be, direct care workers know what they are. Thus, being proactive and creative means getting the right people to the tables discussing change.

We know that a big part of the problem in attracting and retaining direct care staff has been inappropriate funding. But it is not the only ill ailing our field. Direct care workers need more than just salary increases. They need training, professional opportunity — and recognition as equal members of the team. So let's go out and get the money from our states and our legislatures, and when we do, let us remember the pleas we cry out year after year: "We need more money to hire and retain direct care workers. They work evenings, weekends and holidays. They spend the most time with the children and have the greatest potential impact on their lives. They are important to the kids."

Let's actually make these folks important and equal members of our own individual teams.

(Portions of this chapter were derived by an article written by the author that first appeared in the November 2001 edition of *Common Ground.*)

CHAPTER TEN

Educational Needs for Children in Care

"Far away there in the sunshine are my highest aspirations. I may not reach them, but I can look up and see their beauty, believe in them, and try to follow where they lead."

Louisa May Alcott

This last chapter will focus on current educational trends regarding children in care, as well as ways that the field can help these youth in their academic pursuits. I have chosen to end the book with this chapter because the educational needs of children in care are vital, yet frequently overlooked. Furthermore, there is a role that residential programs can play to ensure these services are provided appropriately to children in their charge.

As discussed in earlier chapters, a child's safety and permanence have been addressed nationally. The Adoption and Safe Families Act of 1997 (as well as the Child Abuse Prevention and Treatment Act of 1996, or CAPTA) are examples of this. However, the arrangements that are made (or not made) to address a child's education are hardly a major consideration (Joiner, 2001). Whatever the reasons may be for this "lack of concern" for a child's schooling, our field must begin to see this as a real need in the child's placement.

By looking at the current trends, we will be able to discern where (and what) educational services are lacking. (Sometimes this means looking past a child's behavior to ensure their educational needs are met.) We will then be able to discern ways to address deficiencies. And, as in other areas in our work, we have plenty to keep us busy. This is the exciting thing about our field!

CURRENT TRENDS IN THE EDUCATION OF CHILDREN AND YOUTH IN CARE

A collaboration project between the Child Welfare League of America (CWLA) and the Permanency Planning for Children Department of the National Council of Juvenile and Family Court

Judges, in consultation with Casey Family Programs, has provided concrete data regarding educational trends for children in placement. In *Improving Educational Outcomes for Youth in Care* (2002), an executive summary of the aforementioned project, authors Elisabeth Yu, Pamela Day and Millicent Williams, note the following statistics:

- 26% - 40% of youth in care repeated one or more grades.
- 30% - 96% of students in care were below grade level in reading and math.
- 37% - 80% of youth had not completed high school even after leaving care.
- 30% - 41% of youth received special education (number may be underreported).

Yu, et al. (2002) conclude that some of the driving factors to these statistics being what they are include:

1. *Placement Stability:* Changes in placement often cause changes in schools, and academic performance suffers as a result of this disruption (Yu, et al., 2002). The authors note children in care experience an average of three to four placements, often resulting in school changes, and that:

   > Each move to a new school forces students in care to adjust to new curricula, teachers, academic demands, group norms and school peers. Placement disruptions make it difficult for students in care to receive timely assessments, obtain continuous educational services, and have accurate and complete school histories (p. viii).

2. *Lack of collaboration/communication between child welfare agencies and schools.*
3. *Schools stifle a student's educational progress by resisting or delaying admission.*
4. *Schools fail to recognize an individualized educational plan (IEP).*
5. *Schools fail to provide a social environment that accepts students in care.*
6. *Teachers are not empathetic, or sensitive to the needs of students in care.*

(The next section of the chapter will address this last item in greater detail. It is important to do this because, just as direct care workers must be empathetic to the child's needs, teachers can only help students if they are respectful of them.)

Youth that do not receive proper education suffer dire consequences as they continue their life's journey. It was noted earlier that 37% - 80% of youth in care do not complete their high school education. This sad statistic belies the fact that a college degree is essential for providing better job opportunities and higher earnings (Yu, et al., 2002). A 1997 study by Sum, Fogg, and Fogg concluded that at age 24 only 35% of high school dropouts were employed full-time, whereas 87% of college graduates were employed full-time. Furthermore, the annual earnings in 1999 for those who had completed high school was $24,572, which contrasts the annual earnings of college graduates (bachelor's level) being $45,678 (Newburger & Curry, 2000a.)

These statistics tell us that education is the best chance for youth in care succeeding in the adult world (Coeyman, 2001; Yu, et al. 2002). When we consider that some adolescents in placement are discharged from care at the age of 18, their schooling becomes even more important. With the numbers of youth in care not completing high school, and being what they are; an alarm must be sounded in our field. We have to find ways to make sure that these youngsters receive the proper educational services. And, we have to encourage them to continue their studies past the high school level. (In my home state of Rhode Island, youth in care can attend college tuition free. I am happy to note that this initiative is occurring in many other states as well.)

LOOKING PAST A CHILD'S BEHAVIOR TO ENSURE THEIR EDUCATION

As noted earlier, teachers can help students by being sensitive to each student's individual needs. Those of us who have worked in the field know that this is sometimes easier said than done. It requires that all teachers make a Herculean effort in this area if we are to help youth in care succeed in their academic pursuits.

This publication has labored to make the point that we work with difficult youth. Their behavior does not always endear them to us. That is why another point this book has repeatedly made is that children should not be viewed solely by their behavior but, rather, by what the need behind their behavior is telling us. We should be cognizant to view the internal needs of the child in addition to (and even more so than) the external behavior they are presenting.

In their sound text, *Discipline Without Tears* (1972) Rudolph Driekurs and Pearl Cassel conclude:

> A child needs encouragement like a plant needs sun and water. Unfortunately, those who need encouragement most, get it the least because they behave in such a way that our reaction to them pushes them further into discouragement and rebellion (p. 49).

This statement perfectly describes the relationship that some staff, including teachers, (intentionally or unintentionally), develop with the children in their charge. What we have to remember is that children and youth in residential placement try to push adults away from them. The temptation to allow this to occur must be resisted. When they succeed in pushing caregivers away from them, it reconfirms to the child their belief that adults don't care about them and/or that they are no good. That is why we cannot foster estranged relationships with any child in care (residential or school setting).

In addition to a child's behavior, teachers must also be sensitive to a youngster's learning style. As covered in earlier portions of this book, some children learn differently, whether they are in residential placement or not. David Smith (2001) quotes Walt Disney, one of the most creative persons of the 20th century, and one who did not have an indulgent childhood, as proclaiming:

> Humans (have) learned life's lessons by seeing real things or pictures with their eyes ages before they began learning through written or spoken words, so it is not strange that some still learn readily by pictures (p. 163).

Disney's remark reaffirms that we do not all learn in traditional ways. This can be particularly true with children in care. Teachers are charged with the task of helping these youth learn, sometimes amidst defiant behavior that can be caused by their frustration in not be able to complete tasks that other children may have mastered years earlier.

John Dewey is beyond a doubt the American educator who influenced our thinking about academics in this country (Garhart Mooney, 2000). In *Experience and Education* (1938) he echoes the thinking of Walt Disney. He felt that it was important for teachers to observe children and to determine from these observations what kind of educational experiences the children are interested in and ready for (Garhart Mooney, 2000). An innovative pioneer (born in 1859) Dewey believed that teachers should ask themselves the following questions

when planning educational activities for children:
- How does this expand on what the child already knows?
- How will this educational activity help the child grow?
- What skills are being developed?
- How will these educational activities prepare the children to live more fully?

Dewey's work, which is still all-important in the historical study of American education, is significant to this chapter because of the last bullet. Perhaps youth in care need to be assisted to "live more fully" more than any other student. These children need to overcome traumatic pasts – and their educational needs are just as important as their clinical treatment is. Teachers can play a fundamental role in helping each child "live more fully" by meeting them at their level of academic need.

Teachers who work with children living in residential placement have just as important a job as the direct care workers that care for youngsters in the milieu. That is why training for educators is just as necessary. Even if a teacher in a special educational setting has the proper degree, it does not mean that they are prepared to work with these often- difficult children. Some teachers may not be as ready as they need to be for the overt behaviors youth in care can present. Casting aside the most problematic child is not the answer. Additional and specialized training can help teachers greatly.

As had been stated in chapter two, some direct care staff members may not be "cut out" to work with difficult children in residential care. The same is true of teachers who work with difficult students, including youth in care. There is no shame in this. These youngsters can test limits and their behaviors can entice even devoted teachers to cast the most annoying child aside. If a teacher does not feel they can hold all the children in their class in the same esteem, they may be in the wrong field. No child should be willingly allowed to fall through the (academic) cracks.

Schools and Residential Treatment Agencies

Some still may be asking, "Why is this chapter included in this book?" It is incorporated into this publication because:

1. Residential programs can assist schools in their work with children in care.
2. In some agencies there is an overlap amongst residential and academic services.

How Can Residential Providers Assist Schools

Children in out-of-home placement have higher absentee and tardy rates and are twice as likely (37% versus 16%) to have dropped out of high school than youth who are not in care (Blome, 1997; Joiner, 2001). Reports from a multitude of states show that children in care change schools during the year, miss weeks (or entire months) of school at a time due to placement instability and/or schools being resistant to their admission, and teachers often find it difficult to give extra attention to students with special needs (Yu, et al., 2002). Some schools will enroll the child for a limited day because of past behavioral problems, issue repeated suspensions that could lead to expulsion, and enroll a child with an IEP but do not recognize it (Yu, et al., 2002). These practices have led children in care to openly state that they do not feel their teachers provide them with equitable treatment (Altshuler, 1997b; Yu, et al., 2002).

Based on the aforementioned information, there are a number of ways in which residential providers (and the State or County Department) can help children in care receive proper educational services. According to Yu, et al. (2002) some hopeful practices include:

- A commitment to keep children and youth in the same school.
- Training workers to consider school stability when making placement changes.
- Training residential staff (and foster parents) to be educational advocates.
- Educating schools about the needs of children in care.
- Facilitating interaction between all parties involved in a student's life.

Schools That are a Part of Residential Treatment Programs Should Have an Advantage

Because there is an overlap of services, nowhere should we expect teachers to be more attentive to a child's academic needs than in residential treatment facilities (chapter two) or other agencies that incorporate residential and educational services in their care of children. These school programs have the benefit of working with the residential team in helping youth master their academic endeavors. These teachers can converse with residential staff members to discuss a child's behavior and develop strategies to help that youngster in the classroom. In these instances, the schools should be in a better (meaning more advantageous) position to work with even the most difficult children in the classroom setting.

Having once worked in a residential treatment program, I, myself, had worked closely with teachers in our agency's special educational program. I had also filled in on occasion as a teacher-assistant and completed an undergraduate internship as a crisis intervention worker at a special-ed school. The work in the school setting was fantastic. However, one of the things I noticed was that some of the teachers did not always view the residential staff as part of the team, and, conversely, some residential workers felt the teachers' job was far too easy in comparison to their labor with children in the milieu. Both of these misconceptions underscore the need for open lines of communication.

Aside from my experience in the special education setting for youth in care, I have had the opportunity to review an abundance of literature, visit other special education schools, talk with a number of teachers and principles, and listen to youth in care. Especially in schools that are components of residential treatment programs, it is this author's belief that the following recommendations can be incorporated into a school's *classroom musts*:

- ❏ Children should not be separated from the class for an endless amount of time.
- ❏ Time-outs should be for a specific amount of time, and not open-ended.
- ❏ Dialogue and team meetings with residential staff members should be expected.
- ❏ If a teacher is not relating well with a particular child, he/she should address this issue with their supervisor and discern a solution.
- ❏ On-going training opportunities for teachers should be made available.
- ❏ Carry-over consequences (school to residence, vice versa) should not be arbitrary.

❏ The classroom should be orderly.

Regarding carry-over consequences, this practice is not something to be taken lightly. The problem is that it can be easy for a frustrated teacher to say "I'm going to give you carry-over restriction if you don't calm down." Carry-over consequences are a serious message to a youngster. Holding a child accountable for something he/she did in school is appropriate. (A child living at home with his/her parents would most likely face a consequence if he/she acted violently at school, destroyed school property, failed to ever complete homework assignments, etc.) However, an agency should have protocols and guidelines for when and how carry-over consequences are to be administered. First and foremost, carry-over consequences should not be administered without a team discussion.

To reiterate my affirmation, I will relate the example of Sammy and the salami sandwiches. (This is actually an example of a carry-over consequence from the residence into school.)
Sammy had been acting up in the residential program and was becoming highly aggressive towards staff and his peers. One night at supper, when he didn't like the meal (chicken parmesan), he hurled it across the dining room, sending it crashing against the wall. The agency decided that since Sammy was a danger at the dinner table, and since he didn't like "good" meals, he would have to eat soft and "basic" foods. This meant he could only have salami and cheese sandwiches for all of his meals. (Why not give just give him the same meals his peers were eating, but only on paper plates?) If he was behaving well Sammy could have peanut butter and toast for breakfast. His teacher in school found out that this carried over into the school program from a residential staff member.

Not only was this carry-over consequence a bit vindictive (making the child eat the same "bare minimum" meal over and over is the sort of thing the court of public opinion, i.e. taxpayers, would crucify our field for), but also it was a case where others made a decision on a carry-over consequence without the input of the entire team. (The residential team and administration made the decision solely.) The other issue was that the teacher had a problem with the meal policy and lost the opportunity to voice her opinion in the proper forum. That is why communication between team members is all so important. In the case of carry-over consequences, how can one setting make a decision without input from the other setting that will be expected to adhere to the particulars of a carry-over consequence?

This last bullet in the *classroom musts* highlights (orderly classroom settings) is also important. Just as the milieu needs to be orderly, the classroom should be as well. Books simply cast on shelves and desks, scraps of paper scattered about the floor, and even overturned desks left that way for hours while a youngster has been removed from the classroom setting, all convey the message to students that they are just the same messy kids living the same old messy life. Teachers must provide wonderful sensory experiences for children (this includes the site of an orderly classroom), for creating the proper (orderly) environment is just as important a part of teaching as knowing how to select the right children's books from the library (Garhardt Mooney, 2000).

Promising Practices to Address Deficient Areas

We know that in special education and public school settings, children in out-of-home placements are *falling through the educational cracks*. But there are things that we all can be doing to make sure that this does not happen. The work by Yu, et al. (2002) reviews some ways in which states within the child welfare system are helping meet the educational needs of youth in care. Most of the data has been gathered form a 1999 report issued by the U.S. General Accounting Office. Some of these promising practices include:
- Forty-one states reported that they assisted youth with preparing for or completing education or vocational training.
- Thirty-three states helped youth pursue postsecondary education.
- Twenty-one states awarded tuition waivers for college or vocation schools.
- Twenty states helped pay for other educational expenses (books, exam fees, etc.)

Other ways that the child welfare agency can help improve educational outcomes for youth in care, include:
- Making a commitment to keep youth in the same school while a child is in out-of-home care (Dougherty, 2001).
- Training social workers to consider the effects of a school change when making decisions about a placement change

(Blome, 1997). Agencies should also be flexible in retaining youth, when possible, through the end of a school year.
- Watching for biases that expect lower achievement from youth in care and promote a high school diploma as the final degree for these youth (Blome, 1997).

The Future Can Be As Bright As We Want It To Be For Youth in Care

Youth in care do not have to be maintained-only in the school environment. Their teachers should have higher expectations for them than that. The sky is the limit in most cases. When we help children in care realize their unlimited potential, we are making our own future brighter. It is something that we all have a vested interest in.

I have had the good fortune of caring for youth who have moved onto better lives. One of the greatest honors that I have had is in working (in the professional sense) with two individuals who are graduates of the child welfare system. Currently, one of these individuals is in the second year of college, working towards a Bachelor's degree, and eventually a Masters, in Social Work. The other individual is a working mom, who is completing her third year of undergraduate education towards a law degree. Both individuals are students and work part-time in our field, helping youth in care realize their own potential. These two young adults have proven that no matter what the past has brought, anything is possible – the sky truly is the limit!

Teachers and direct care workers: each of these positions plays an important role in helping youth in care improve educational outcomes. It is why our jobs are so important in society. We truly can help children in care reach their optimal potential – even in the classroom.

FINAL THOUGHTS

There is an oversized coffee mug that sits upon a shelf on the credenza in my office. The mug holds a picture of Mickey Mouse, in a suit and tie, working at a computer with the letters C.E.O. under the picture. One day a Board Member happened to be in my office and saw the mug, making the assumption that the letters meant chief executive officer. This person then told me, "You're not a C.E.O." What this individual didn't see was the small writing under the letters, which explained that C.E.O. meant *Creative, Energetic, Optimistic.*

I informed the Board Member, "I am C.E.O."

This example sheds light on something that is sorely lacking in our work. That is the need to think differently; to think outside the box; to see the canvas as having great potential in its color schemes instead of being painted in blacks and grays. We are amidst change, thus we have to be able to think and work proactively. One of my favorite things to say is "We can't envision building skyscrapers when the land is occupied by dinosaurs." We have got to rid ourselves of any archaic thinking and leap into the evolving "business" of helping youth in care, and their families, in any ways possible.

The mark that this text has aimed for has included providing workers with the basics of residential care for children. These "basics" included brief forays into theory, philosophical concepts, and current initiatives engaging our field. Attempts were also made to reiterate themes important to our work. And, of course, one of the main themes is that we sometimes have to change the way we approach things.

In the mode of looking at things differently, I suggest that residential staff members have unlimited power and control – and that's the way it should be. Remember that power and control can mean different things. To children it might mean that adults are free to exert dominion over them. To executives, or other administrative-types, it can mean trying to micro-manage, assert authority over, or bully other individuals. Either definition is negative and contemptuous. It is not the definition of power and control I feel anyone strives towards.

My definition of power and control for residential staff members is one of hope, and is highly positive in nature. I assert that residential staff members have the power and control to:

- Help children overcome the trauma of their past to realize bright futures.
- Aid children and families in re-uniting, or establish the best relationship possible.
- Advocate for children and youth who sorely need supporters.
- Educate politicians, schools, and communities as to the needs of children in care.
- Give those often forgotten by our society a place to belong to (and be safe).
- Most importantly, residential staff members have the chance to shape the future.

This is such an awesome power to have and it must be safeguarded as a worker's most sacred of duties. How many other jobs are there in this world where someone has the chance to positively shape the future? Conversely, if this power is not taken seriously, or used correctly, residential staff members can help to sustain the status quo for children in care – they can see to it that the future is darker for us all.

Respecting the work that we do, residential work with children, should be the legacy that we leave behind.

APPENDIX

Additional Resources

This appendix lists potential resources on some of topics covered in the text. (The bibliography also provides a comprehensive list of sources that were used in the preparation of this work.)

Accreditation
The following bodies offer accreditation of residential programs:

CARF – "The Rehabilitation Accreditation Commission"
4891 E. Grant Road
Tucson, AZ 85712
Phone: (520) 325-1044

Council on Accreditation
120 Wall Street, 11th Floor
New York, NY 10005
Phone: (212) 797-3000

Joint Commission on Accreditation of Healthcare Organizations (JCAHO)
One Renaissance Boulevard
Oakbrook Terrace, IL 60181
Phone: (630) 792-5000

Books Pertinent to Children's Residential Placement
Amongst the multitude of books pertinent to our work are:

Beating the Odds: Crime Poverty and Life in the Inner City, McNamara (1999)
Can be ordered through the Child Welfare League of America Press at www.cwla.org

In Whose Best Interest? One Child's Odyssey, A Nation's Responsibility, Seita, (1996)
This book can be ordered at www.Amazon.com

The Gus Chronicles: Reflections From an Abused Kid, Appelstein (1994)
Gus Chronicles II: Reflections From A Kid Who Has Been Abused, Appelstein (2002)
Both of these books can be ordered at www.charliea.com or at www.Amazon.com

The Lost Boy, Pelzer (1998). All of Dave Pelzer's books can be found in any bookstore or can be ordered at www.Amazon.com

Child Welfare Issues and Information (National)
Child Welfare League of America
National Headquarters
440 First Street NW, Third Floor
Washington, DC 20001-2085
Phone: (202) 638-2952
www.cwla.org

CWLA Regional Offices

CWLA Mid-Atlantic Office
Board of Child Care
3330 Gaither Road
Baltimore, MD 21244
(410) 496-5624

CWLA Mid-West Office
125 South Wacker Drive
14th Floor
Chicago, IL 60606
(312) 424-6843

CWLA Southern Office
12020-D North Shore Dr.
Reston, VA 20190
(703) 787-9121

CWLA Mountain/Plains Office
455 Sherman Street, Suite 550
Denver, CO 80203
(720) 570-9488

CWLA New England Office
300 Congress Street, Suite 305
Quincy, MA 02169
(617) 769-4020

Pertaining to children's residential placement, another good resource is the AACRC:

American Association of Children's Residential Centers
51 Monroe Place, Suite 1603
Rockville, MD 20850
(301) 738-6460
www.aacrc-dc.org

**CONSULATION SERVICES
(For Boards, Managed Care, Networking)**

Child Welfare League of America
National Center for Consultation and Professional Development
Phone: (202) 942-0287
e-mail: nccpd@cwla.org

Another good resource, especially in the Northeast, is:

New England Network for Child, Youth and Family Services
25 Stow Road
Boxboro, MA 01719
Phone: (978) 266-1998
www.nenetwork.org

Crisis Intervention Models

There are many models in crisis intervention that are currently being marketing. It is suggested that agencies conduct a thorough investigation on these models. The models listed below are those the author has familiarity with:

Crisis Prevention Institute
3315-K 124th Street
Brookfield, WI 53005
(800) 558-8978
ww.crisisprevention.com

Handle With Care
184 McKinstry Road
Gardiner, NY 12525
(845) 256-0094
(607) 255-4837

Therapeutic Crisis Intervention
Cornell University
MVR Hall
Ithica, NY 14853-4401
http://ed.cornell.edu/rccp/

Ethical Codes

In addition to the *code of ethics* for residential workers found in this text, the following professional associations (psychologists, educators and social workers) also have their own code of ethics:

American Psychological Association
Ethics Office
750 First Street, NE
Washington, D.C. 20002
(202) 336-5930
www.apa.org

National Educational Association
1201 16th Street, NW
Washington, DC 20036
(202) 833-4000
www.nea.org

The National Association of Social Workers
750 First Street, NE
Washington, D.C. 20002-4241
(202) 408-8600
www.naswdc.org

Staff Development Programs

There are numerous staff development programs across the country. Some of the national training centers/programs are listed below.

Child Welfare League of America
Walker Trieschman Center Division
300 Congress Street, Suite 305
Quincy, MA 02169
(617) 769-4008
e-mail: wtc@cwla.org

The University of Oklahoma - Tulsa National Resource Center for
Youth Services (NRCYS) Schusterman Center
4502 E. 41st Street, Bldg. 4W Tulsa, OK 74135
Phone: 918-660-3700

Complimenting this list is the *Association of Child and Youth Care Practice* (ACYCP). The ACYCP is attempting to define national standards for worker certification. For more information on this project please contact the ACYCP at:

Association for Child & Youth Care Practice
c/o Child & Youth Care Learning Center
University of Milwaukee-Wisconsin
161 W. Wisconsin Avenue, Suite 6000
Milwaukee, WI 53203
(414) 227-3354
www.acycp.org

TRAUMA WORK WITH CHILDREN

There are many good resources in our individual states that can be utilized to assist in your work with traumatized children. The internet is also provides an avenue for further resources. Just a few of these sites are listed here:

Advocate Family Care Network
www.advocatehealth.com
This site contains links to numerous resources.

Psychological Trauma: Treatment, Resources and Biology
www.psychinnovations.com
This site contains links to dozens of articles and program models.

Risking Connection
www.riskingconnection.com
This site contains training curriculums and information on trauma work with children.

BIBLIOGRAPHY

Allen, D. (2002). (2002). Tuesday's Child. *Adoption Rhode Island Newsletter*, p. 2.

Altshuler, S. (1997b). *The Educational Experiences of Children in Foster Care: The Perceptions of Teachers, Foster Parents, and Children.* (Final Report) Urbana, IL: University of Illinois at Urbana-Champaign.

Appelstein, C. (1998). *No Such Thing as a Bad Kid.* Weston, MA: The Gifford School.

Appelstein, C. (1994). *The Gus Chronicles: Reflections From an Abused Kid.* Needham, MA: Albert E. Trieschman Center.

Appelstein, C. (2002). *The Gus Chronicles II: Reflections From A Kid Who Has Been Abused.* Cranston, RI: RICORP.

Appelstein, C. (2001). RICORP Journal. *Welcome to Residential Counseling,* p. 19-27.

Association of Child and Youth Care Practice (1995). *Ethics of Child and Youth Care Professionals.* (On-line) Available: http://www.pitt.edu/~mattgly/CYCethics.html (2002 February 14).

Association of Child and Youth Care Practice (1995). *North American Certification Project.* (On-line) Available: http://www.acycp.org/nacp.htm (2002 May 3).

Barbell, K. & Freundlich, M. (2001). *Foster Care Today.* Washington, D.C.: Casey Family Programs.

Berger, K. (1994). *The Developing Person Through the Life Span.* New York, NY: Worth Publishers.

Biller, H. & Meredith, D.L. (1975). *Father Power.* New York, NY: Doubleday Anchor Books.

Biller, H. & Solomon, R. (1986). *Child Maltreatment and Paternal Deprivation.* Lexington, MA: Lexington Books.

Blome, W. (1997). What happens to foster kids: Educational experiences of a random sample of foster care youth and a matched group of non-foster care youth. *Child and Adolescent Social Work Journal, 14,* 41-53.

Bloom, R. (1993). When Staff Members Sexually Abuse Children in Residential Care. *Residential Treatment For Children and Youth, 11 (2),* p. 89-106.

Bloom, R., Denton, I.R., Caflish, C. (1991). Institutional Sexual Abuse: A Crisis in Trust. *Contributions to Residential Treatment, AACRC,* p. 48-49.

Brohl, K. (1996). *Working With Traumatized Children: A Handbook for Healing.* Washington, D.C.: CWLA Press.

Carl, D. & Jurkoviv, G.J. (1983). Agency triangles: Problems in agency-family relationships. *Family Process, 22,* 441-451.

CASA (1996). What is Cultural Competence? (Online). Available: http://www.casanet. org/ library/culture/competence.htm (2002 March 28)

CASSA (1999). The Art of Being a Good Listener. *Canadian Association of Student Activity Advisors.* (On-line). Available: http:// www.casaa-resources.net/resources/sourcebook/acquiring-leader.../listening-skills.htm (2002 March 12)

Charles, G., Coleman, H., & Matheson, J. (1993). Staff Reactions to Young People Who Have Been Sexually Abused. *The Management of Sexuality in Residential Treatment,* p. 9-21.

Child Welfare League of America (2001). Cultural Competence. *Child Welfare League of America.* (Online). Available: http://www.cwla.org/programs/culturalcompetence.htm (2002 March 12)

Child Welfare League of America (2002). Family Preservation Services Fact Sheet. *Child Welfare League of America.* (Online). Available: http://www.cwla.org/programs/familypractice/fampresfactsheet.htm (2002 June 27)

Child Welfare League of America (2002). What Works: Research on Family Preservation Services. *Child Welfare League of America.* (Online). Available: http://www.cwla.org/programs/family practice/fampresworks.htm (2002 June 26)

Ciliberti, P. (1998). An Innovative Family Preservation Program in an African American Community: Longitudinal Analysis. *Family Preservation Journal, 3(2),* 45-72.

CMHA (2001). Coping With Stress: Tips for Dealing With Stress and Tension. *Canadian Mental Health Association.* (Online). Available: http://www3.sympatico.ca/cmha.toronto/stressn.html (2002 April 28).

Coeyman, M. (2001). Lost in the Shuffle. *Christian Science Monitor.* Available:http//www.publicbroadcast.net/wnyc/news/other/article/html (2002 December 1).

Dewey, J. (1938). *Experience and Education.* New York, NY: Collier Macmillan.

Dreikurs, R. & Cassel, P. (1972). *Discipline Without Tears: What to do With Children who Misbehave.* New York, NY: Hawthorn Books, Inc.

Dobson, J. (1992). *The New Dare to Discipline.* Wheaton, IL: Tyndale House Publishers.

Dougherty, S. (2001). *Toolboxes for Permanency: Toolbox No. 2 Expanding the Role of Foster Parents in Achieving Permanency.* Washington, D.C.: CWLA Press

Edelman, H. (1994). *Motherless Daughters*. Reading, MA: Addison Wesley Publishing Company.

Education Development (2002). *The Dreikurs Model*. (Online). Available: http://www.solscitt.net/sgfl/teaching/discplan/dreik.htm (2002 July 30).

Elkind, D. (2001). *The Hurried Child*. Reading, MA: Addison-Wesley Publishing Co.

Erikson, E. (1985). *Childhood and Society*. New York, NY: W.W. Norton Company.

Flavell, J. (1963). *The Developmental Psychology of Jean Piaget*. Princeton, NJ: Van Nostrand.

Foy, D. (1992). *Treating PTSD: Cognitive-Behavioral Strategies*. New York, NY: Guilford Press.

Freundlich, M. (1997). The future of adoption for children in foster care. *Journal of Children and Poverty, 3 (2)*, 33-61.

Garhardt Mooney, C. (2000). *Theories of Childhood*. St. Paul, MN: Redleaf Press.

Grebstein, L.C. (1986). An eclectic family therapy. *Handbook of Eclectic Therapy* (J. Norcross, Ed.). New York, NY: Brunner/Mazel.

Greenwood, E. (1957). Attributes of a Profession. *Social Work, 3 (2)*, 44-45.

Goldstein, A. & McGinnis, E. (1997). *Skillstreaming the Adolescent*. Champaign, IL: Research Press.

Hoffman, M.L. (1996). The role of the father in moral internalization. *The Role of the Father in Child Development* (M.E. Lamb, Ed.) New York, NY: John Wiley and Sons.

Joiner, L. (2001). Reaching out to children in care. *American School Board Journal, 188,* 30-37.

Keegan, R. (1996). *The Evolving Self.* Cambridge, MA: Harvard University Press.

Kohlberg, L. (1963). Development of children's orientation towards a moral order. Sequencing in the development of moral thought. *Vita Humana, 6,* 11-36.

Krueger, M. (1988). *Intervention Techniques for Child/Youth Care Workers.* Washington, D.C.: CWLA Press

Lytton, H. (1979). Disciplinary encounters between young boys and their mothers and fathers: Is there a contingency system? *Developmental Psychology, 15,* 256-268.

Maslow, A. (1985). *Motivation and Personality.* New York, NY: Harper & Row Publishers.

Matsakis, A. (1998). *Trust After Trauma.* Oakland, CA: New Harbinger Publications.

McNamara, R. (1999). *Beating the Odds: Crime, Poverty and Life in the Inner City.* Washington, D.C.: CWLA Press

Meezan, W. & McCroskey, J. (1996). Improving Family Functioning through Family Preservation Services: Results of the Los Angeles Experiment. *Family Preservation Journal, Winter 1996,* 9-29.

Merriam-Webster (1997). *The Merriam-Webster Dictionary.* Springfield, MA: Merriam-Webster, Inc.

Micucci, J. (1998). *The Adolescent in Family Therapy.* New York, NY: Guilford Press.

Nash, K. (1999). *Cultural Competence: A Guide for Human Service Agencies.* Washington, D.C.: CWLA Press.

National Association of School Psychologists (2001). Helping Children Cope with Loss (Online) Available: http://www.nasponline.org/NEAT/grief.html (2002, March 18).

National Child Welfare Resource Center for Family Centered Practice (2000). A New Era of Family-Centered Practice. *Best Practice, Next Practice: family Centered Child Welfare, 1 (1),* 1-15.

Newburger, E. & Curry, A. (2000a). *Educational attainment in the United States.* (U.S. Census Bureau Publication No. P20-356) Washington, D.C.: U.S. Department of Commerce.

Paddock, D. (2002). Grief and Loss Issues for Adopted Children: Caring Adults Can Make a World of Difference. *Families With a Difference* (Online). Available: http://www.adopting.org/DeePaddock/html/grief_loss_.html (2002 March 10)

Perry, B. (1996). The Impact of Abuse and Neglect on the Developing Brain. *Scholastic On-line Teachers.* (On-line) Available: htttp://teacher.scholastic.com/professional/bruceperry/abuse neglect.htm (2002 July 12)

Peterson, M. (1992). *At Personal Risk.* New York, NY: Norton Press.

Piaget, J. (1973). *The Child and Reality.* New York, NY: Viking Press.

Pincus, J. & Tucker, G. (1992). *Behavioral Neurology.* New York, NY: Oxford University Press.

Prevent Child Abuse America (2001). *Current Trends in Child Abuse: Prevention, Reporting, and Fatalities.* Chicago, IL: Prevent Child Abuse America.

Resources for Cross Cultural Health (1999). Measuring Cultural Competence in Healthcare. *HHS Office of Minority Health,* p. 1-5.

Schwartz, I.M., AuClaire, P., & Harris, L.J. (1991). Family Preservation Services as an Alternative to the Out-of-Home Placement of Adolescents: The Hennepin County Experience. *Family Preservation Services: Research and Evaluation.* (D.E. Biegel & K. Wells, Eds.). Newbury Park, CA: Sage Press, 33-46.

Seita, J., Mitchel, M. & Tobin, C. (1996). *In Whose Best Interest? One Child's Odyssey, A Nation's Responsibility.* Elizabethtown, PA: Continental Press.

Sinanoglu, P. & Malluccio, A. (1988). *Parents of Children in Placement: Perspectives and Programs.* Washington, D.C.: CWLA Press.

Smith, D. (2001). *The Quotable Walt Disney.* New York, NY: Disney Editions.

Stevens-Long & Common, M. (1992). *Adult Life.* Mountain View, CA: Mayfield Publishing Company.

Sum, A., Fogg, N. & Fogg, N. (1997). Confronting the demographic challenge: Future labor market prospects of out-of-school young adults. *A Generation of Challenge: Pathways to Success for Urban Youth,* (A. Sum, S. Mangum, E. DeJesus, G. Walker, D. Gruber, M. Pines, et al., Eds.). Baltimore, MD: Sar Levitan Center for Social Policy Studies, p. 13-44.

Tartara, T. (1993). *Characteristics of children in substitute and adoptive care: A statistical summary of the VCIS National Child Welfare Data Base.* Washington, D.C.: American Public Welfare Association.

Thomas, R. (1992). *Comparing Theories of Child Development.* Belmont, CA: Wadsworth Publishing Company.

Tortora, G. & Evans R. (1990). *Principles of Human Physiology.* New York, NY; Harper & Row Publishers.

Trieschman, A., Whittaker, J. & Brendtro, L. (1969). *The Other Twenty-Three Hours.* New York, NY: Aldine De Gruyter, Co.

University of Oklahoma, National Resource Center. (1988). Creating a Positive Environment. *University of Oklahoma Advanced Training Course For Residential Child Care Workers.* Tulsa, OK: University of Oklahoma.

U.S. Census Bureau. (1999). *Statistical Abstract of the United States: 1999.* Washington, D.C.: U.S. Department of Commerce, Economics and Statistics Division, Census Bureau.

U.S. Census Bureau. (2001a). *Overview of Race and Hispanic Origin.* Washingston, D.C.: U.S. Department of Commerce, Economics and Statistics Administration, Census Bureau.

U.S. Census Bureau. (2001b). *Methodology and assumptions for the population projects of the United States: 1999-2100.* (Population Division Working Paper No. 38). Washington, D.C.: U.S. Department of Commerce, Economics and Statistics Administration, Census Bureau

U.S. Department of Health and Human Services (2000). *Rethinking Child Welfare Practice Under the Adoption and Safe Families Act of 1997.* Washington, D.C: U.S. Government Printing Office.

U.S. Department of Health and Human Services. (2000a). *The AFCARS report: Interim estimates for fiscal year 1998.* (Online).Available: http:/www.acf.dhhhs.gov/programs/cb/stats/tarreport/rtp04003/ar0400.html (2002 January 12).

U.S. Department of Health and Human Services. (2000b). *Child welfare outcomes 1998: Annual report.* Washington, D.C.: U.S. Department of Health and Human Services, Administration for Children and Families, Children's Bureau.

U.S. Department of Health and Human Services. (2001b). *Program instruction: Chafee Foster Care Independence Program, # ACF-CB-PI-01-02.* Washington, D.C.: U.S. Department of Health and Human Services.

U.S. Department of Health and Human Services. (2001c). *AFCARS report #5.* (Online). Available: http:/www.acf.dhhhs.gov/programs/cb/publications/afcars/apr2001.html. (2002, January 14)

U.S. Department of Health and Human Services Office of Minority Health (1999). *Cultural and Linguistically Appropriate Services.* (On-line). Available: http://www.healthlaw.org/pubs/199909Ling Standards.html (2002 March 28)

U.S. General Accounting Office (1999). *Foster care: Effectiveness of Independent Living Services Unknown.* Washington, D.C.: U.S. Government Printing Office.

U.S. House of Representatives, Committee on Ways and Means. (1994). *1994 green book: Overview of entitlement programs.* Washington, D.C.: Government Printing Office.

Wallerstein, J.S. & Kelly, J.B. (1996). *Surviving the Breakup: How Children and Parents Cope With Divorce.* New York, NY: Basic Books.

Weltner, L. (1988). *No Place Like Home.* New York, NY: William Morrow Company.

Whitman, C. (1991). *Win the Whining War & Other Skirmishes.* Los Angeles, CA: Perspective Publishing.

Wichman, F. (2002). *In Search of Rudolph Dreikurs.* (Online). Available: http://web.csuchico.edu/^ah24/dreikurs.htm (2002 August 2).

Wisconsin Education Association Council. (1996). *A Symphony of Learning Styles.* (On-line). Available: http://www.weac.org/kids/june96/styles.htm (2002 July 9).

Wulczyn, F.H., Harden, A.W., & George, R.M. (1997). *An update from the multi-state foster care data archive: Foster care dynamics 1983-1994.* Chicago: University of Chicago, The Chapin Hall Center for Children.

Youth Today. (2000). The Rise and Fall of Covenant House. *Youth Today, 1* p. 41-45.

Yu, E., Day, P. & Williams, M. (2002). *Improving Educational Outcomes for Youth in Care: A National Collaboration.* Washington, D.C.: CWLA Press

Zotovich, K. (2000). Helping Children Deal With Loss Through the Journaling Process. *Empowering Caregivers.* (Online). Available: http://www.care-givers.com/pages/carearticles/helping children.html (2002 March 14)

ABOUT THE AUTHOR

James R. Harris Jr. was born in North Kingstown, Rhode Island in 1962. The oldest of five brothers, he graduated from North Kingstown High School in 1980. Mr. Harris holds a Bachelor's degree in Human Development and Family Studies from the *University of Rhode Island.* Upon graduating from URI he was presented the Katzoff Award as the College of Continuing Education's Outstanding Male Graduate. Mr. Harris earned a Master of Arts in Counseling Psychology from *Goddard College* in Vermont.

In 1990 Mr. Harris began his career in children's residential programming when he and his wife became therapeutic foster parents. In 1995 he became residential coordinator at the same agency. While serving in this position, Mr. Harris completed his Master's level internship whereby he served as a counselor at a residential program for adolescents. When he became executive director of the *Rhode Island Council on Residential Programs for Children and Youth* in 1998, Mr. Harris had held positions at every level in the children's residential programming system: from direct care worker to executive.

James R. Harris, Jr. is an experienced trainer and speaker. He is also a proven political lobbyist and tenacious advocate on behalf of children's issues. Still an administrator in the human services field, Mr. Harris is available to provide keynote addresses, workshops, and consultations. Should you wish to contact the author, please visit his website at: www.jh4kidz.com.

NEARI Press Titles

Moving Beyond by Thomas F. Leversee, LCSW (2002). NEARI Press, 70 North Summer Street, Holyoke, MA 01040. Paperback, 88 pages. $20.00 plus shipping and handling. Bulk discounts available.
ISBN# 1-929657-16-1

Moving Beyond Student Manual by Thomas F. Leversee, LCSW (2002). NEARI Press, 70 North Summer Street, Holyoke, MA 01040. Paperback, 52 pages. $10.00 plus shipping and handling. Bulk discounts available.
ISBN# 1-929657-18-8

Growing Beyond by Susan L. Robinson (2002). NEARI Press, 70 North Summer Street, Holyoke, MA 01040. Paperback, approx. 214 pages. $20.00 plus shipping and handling.
ISBN# 1-929657-17-X

Growing Beyond Treatment Manual by Susan L. Robinson (2002). NEARI Press, 70 North Summer Street, Holyoke, MA 01040. Paperback, approx. 40 pages. $15.00 plus shipping and handling.
ISBN# 1-929657-15-3

The Safe Workbook for Youth by John McCarthy and Kathy MacDonald (2001). NEARI Press, 70 North Summer Street, Holyoke, MA 01040. Paperback, 210 pages $20.00 plus shipping and handling.
ISBN# 1-929657-14-5

Paths To Wellness by Robert E. Longo (2001). NEARI Press, 70 North Summer Street, Holyoke, MA 01040. Paperback, 144 pages. $20.00 plus shipping and handling. Bulk discounts available.
ISBN#1-929657-19-6

New Hope For Youth: Experiential Exercises for Children & Adolescents by Robert E. Longo and Deborah P. Longo (2003). NEARI Press, 70 North Summer Street, Holyoke, MA 01040. Paperback,150 pages. $35.00 plus shipping and handling.
ISBN# 1-929657-20-X

Men & Anger: Understanding and Managing Your Anger by Murray Cullen and Robert E. Longo (1999). NEARI Press, 70 North Summer Street, Holyoke, MA 01040. Paperback, 125 pages. $15.00 plus shipping and handling. Bulk discounts available.
ISBN#1-929657-12-9

Who Am I and Why Am I In Treatment by Robert E. Longo with Laren Bays (2000). NEARI Press, 70 North Summer Street, Holyoke, MA 01040. Paperback, 85 pages. $12.00 plus shipping and handling. Bulk discounts available.
ISBN#1-929657-01-3

Why Did I Do It Again & How Can I Stop? by Robert E. Longo with Laren Bays (1999). NEARI Press, 70 North Summer Street, Holyoke, MA 01040. Paperback, 192 pages.$20.00 plus shipping and handling. Bulk discounts available.
ISBN#1-929657-11-0

Enhancing Empathy by Robert E. Longo and Laren Bays (1999). NEARI Press, 70 North Summer Street, Holyoke, MA 01040. Paperback, 77 pages. $12.00 plus shipping and handling. Bulk discounts available.
ISBN#1-929657-04-8

Standards of Care for Youth in Sex Offense Specific Residential Treatment by S. Bengis, A. Brown, R. Longo, B. Matsuda, K. Singer, and J. Thomas (1997, 1998, 1999). NEARI Press, 70 North Summer Street, Holyoke, MA 01040. $40.00 plus shipping and handling. Bulk discounts available.
ISBN# 1-929657-05-6

Respecting Residential Work With Children
by James R. Harris (2003). NEARI Press, 70 North Summer Street, Holyoke, MA 01040. $35.00 plus shipping and handling. Bulk discounts available.
ISBN# 1-929657-21-8

NEARI Press
70 North Summer Street
Holyoke, MA 01040
413.540.0712

Shipping

$4.50 for first copy
50¢ ea. additional copy

Order from:

Whitman Communications, Inc.
PO Box 1220/10 Water Street
Lebanon, NH 03766-4220
1-800-353-3730